The
Divine
RESTING ON MY SHOULDER

The *Divine*
RESTING ON MY SHOULDER

*The Story of How Divine, Mystical
Experiences Brought Me Closer to God*

RICHARD FERGUSON

LifeRich
PUBLISHING

LifeRich Publishing is a registered trademark of
The Reader's Digest Association, Inc.

LifeRich Publishing books may be ordered
through booksellers or by contacting:

LifeRich Publishing
1663 Liberty Drive
Bloomington, IN 47403
www.liferichpublishing.com
1 (888) 238-8637

Because of the dynamic nature of the Internet, any web addresses or
links contained in this book may have changed since publication and
may no longer be valid. The views expressed in this work are solely those
of the author and do not necessarily reflect the views of the publisher,
and the publisher hereby disclaims any responsibility for them.

Any people depicted in stock imagery provided by Thinkstock are
models, and such images are being used for illustrative purposes only.
Certain stock imagery © Thinkstock.

ISBN: 978-1-4897-0278-4 (sc)
ISBN: 978-1-4897-0277-7 (hc)
ISBN: 978-1-4897-0279-1 (e)

Library of Congress Control Number: 2014914829

Printed in the United States of America.

LifeRich Publishing rev. date: 11/10/2014

Contents

Dedication

*T*here have been a few pivotal people in my life who have helped me in so many ways to stay on the path that God has ordained for me. I dedicate this book to these very special people, people of God who are Christians at heart, with all the openness and extraordinary love they have shown me over many years. To say I love them would be an understatement.

I dedicate this book to my lifelong dear friend Br. Tom Bracco, S.J. I have known this wonderful man since I was a junior at Santa Clara University. We have been very close friends ever since. It has been his loving Christian guidance over the past forty-six years that helped me open my heart to God and stay on the spiritual path God ordained for me. Without his guidance and unconditional love, I do not know where I would be today. He has stuck with me through thick and thin and through all the traumatic experiences I have suffered through the years. This is the mark of a true loving friend.

I dedicate this book to Marilyn, my dear late wife of thirty-eight years. She passed away more than five years ago after we both battled her cancer for five years before she passed away. I was her around-the-clock caregiver, which was the hardest, most agonizing, and most loving thing I have ever done. Through her example, she showed me how to sacrifice, love, and live a life of which God would be proud. I can never fully repay this marvelous woman for all the love and good things she did for me during our time together.

I also dedicate this book to the magnificent loving woman I will marry soon after this book is published. Her name is Evangeline. There is no doubt that our coming together as a loving couple is a result of God working in our lives. Thank you, dear Father, for bringing us together and anointing us with your sacred oil of true unending love that will only grow stronger as the years gently flow past us as we gaze into each other's eyes so full of compassionate, romantic love. We will spend the rest of our lives together until our times come and we both will return to that love-filled place we all call heaven. Our love for each other is eternal. True love can never die as love itself forms the true essence of God's creation and will always be with us while God Himself holds us in his arms.

I also dedicate this book to my dear friend Sue, whom I met at Hewlett-Packard almost forty years ago. She is my best friend who walked with me every step of the way when I was going through so many traumatic experiences. She was always there for me, giving me emotional support, love, and complete understanding. It was her friendship, love, and understanding that helped me endure the many painful experiences I went through. I always knew I could count on her and her husband, David, when I got so depressed and became unable to fully take care of myself.

I am truly blessed to have these wonderful people in my life, loving and helping me through the many agonies I endured. I thank all of you from the bottom of my heart for all the things you did for me, the things you said to me, the time you spent with me, and just being with me when I could barely speak a coherent sentence after Marilyn died.

And the last shall be first, so said Jesus Christ. As such, Jesus Christ is first in my heart, and I sing his songs through this imperfect vessel. I dedicate this book to Him, Jesus Christ, creator of the universe. By reading these words in this book, may His love come into your hearts and pave your way closer to Our Father in all his glory.

Introduction

There are those who deny the existence of God. There are those who doubt God. There are those who have faith in God. And then there are those with knowledge of God. I am one of His children who has strong faith in God but who also fervently seeks more and more knowledge of our Heavenly Father. This author seeks neither glory nor recognition by writing books. I seek neither riches nor fame. Rather, I seek more only knowledge of God and the kingdom of God on my knees by prayerfully doing His divine will as best I can during this short life.

This book is unique. It is about what it actually feels like to have real divine mystical experiences and the effect they have on our lives and our heart of hearts. This book is not about near-death experiences. In my life, I have found that you do not need a near-death experience to experience the spiritual realm. You can experience the boundless love of God and Jesus Christ without almost dying. You do not have to almost die to experience spiritual gifts that God wishes to give all of us. I am just a common Christian who loves Jesus Christ. I have never had a near-death experience, but I have had many mystical experiences in my life. I am just like everyone else, but for reasons I do not know, I have experienced many heavenly events in my life. This book is my testimony to you so that you can grow closer to Jesus Christ and

God our Father. The mystical events in my life documented here are proof that heaven exists and that the Bible is true. Only direct truth is written in this book. There is no need to embellish anything. For that matter, fabricating anything about God would be a heinous crime against our creator, something I find repugnant.

This is the story of what the divine mystical has felt like to me when these events occurred and the effect these experiences have had on my life. It is also about just how inexorably intertwined the mystical is with not only my existence on this Earth but also yours. Everything in this universe is connected in deep ways that we do not understand. It is just that most people are closed to this reality. There is so much apathy in modern societies that the soothing caress and whispering love of God goes unnoticed. People are too attached to their iPhones and the latest releases of video games. Therefore, they miss out on what God wants to give us all. I pray that reading this book will open the door of your heart so He can walk through and show you His loving power for each and every one of us.

Whether we perceive them or not, spiritual experiences are an inexorable part of all of our lives. I have personally lived every story in this book. Everything written here is a divine mystical experience that I document to the world as my gift of love for you are also are children of God.

Mystical experiences are a completely different experience from normal life. We perceive the reality around us through a fog of conflicting thoughts, emotions, and other things that constantly compete for our attention. Our five senses give us information about only a tiny slice of the physical reality that exists around us. Even with our sensing only this tiny portion of the physical realm we live in, it blares so loudly at us that we forget some very important truths of God. Our Father does not shout. He does not pound on things to get our attention. No, our heavenly Father comes to us like a gentle whispering breeze of peace and love. He caresses our minds and hearts, being ever faithful in providing all of us what we need if we can tune out the roaring and bellowing ungodly distractions all around us. If we make the effort to tune out the noisy drums of secular culture, we will begin to experience who Jesus Christ is and how close He can be to us in order to save us from hell and bring us to everlasting life. This is our on this earth.

However and wonderfully so, a mystical event is such that all other competing influences in our minds such as emotions and other worldly perceptions are completely blocked out and our focus becomes singular on that one divine experience while it is happening. For a short time, nothing else exists but the one heavenly event in the center of our being. These heavenly mystical experiences bring with them a peace that truly goes beyond understanding. I have had experiences such as this from God, and this is what I will write about—just how it feels to have a mystical event occur in your life. I will relate why they occurred in my life and how each of us can become more attuned to God, who is trying to communicate with us through these magnificent experiences.

I have a confession. I did not want to write this book. It reveals so very much of my inner spiritual life and the wondrous gifts that God has given me. I felt like I would be exposing too much of my private inner spirit life in such a public way. I did not want to do that. So while I pondered if I should write this book, I wrote two other books instead. The first book was titled *A Real Life Christian Spiritual Journey*. The second book was titled *The Story of Human Spiritual Evolution*. During the time I was writing these other books, this book was in the back of my mind.

While writing my third book and during a meditation session, it became clear that I was being instructed by God to stop writing book three and write this book instead. I was not too happy about that. I still resisted. The idea of this book was rattling around in the back of my mind for a number of years, and I still did not want to write it. I consulted with people inside my inner spiritual circle, and the verdict was unanimous. "Rich, write this book!" So I found myself being instructed by the divine, which was confirmed by my closest of spiritual friends. Over a short period of time, I began to realize that this book sprang from the inner most part of my heart and devotion to

God and our Lord Jesus Christ. Somehow, both God and Jesus Christ have chosen me working through the Holy Spirit to write the words that you will read. Like all human endeavors, this will be imperfect, but at the same time, it will reflect not only the will of God but also His desire for all His children to come to know Him better and draw closer to Him in love and devotion. We must know that at every instant of our lives, God is with us far closer than anyone thinks. With God's guidance, I hope to achieve some sort of new revelation for you that will bring His light into your life. If I have, then I am humbled and greatly pleased.

I have been blessed with many mystical experiences. There have been different kinds that occurred at different points in my life and under many different circumstances. Yet all have been unmistakably from God and served their purposes during important points in my life as God was intimately involved with all of them. One divine experience involved Jesus Christ himself.

I have written here what events actually happened, the people involved, the circumstances at the time, and what it really felt like to be involved with and directly experience divine action in my life. I did not embellish anything. The mystical events that occurred stand on their own and are by human terms very joyful and wondrous to read. They are also very loving and reassuring for us all as we all experience our human journey. Most are small communications and very reassuring, while others are extremely significant and life-changing.

What you are about to read are stories about specific mystical events and divine interventions. I have included some events I have not discussed with my friends or relatives. These mystical events fall well outside the normal experiences of human life, and therefore, I kept them to myself except for a few stories I have told to people who are in my inner spiritual circle. I have written about a few in my previous books.

Welcome to the mystical spiritual world. May God bless you and draw you closer to Him through what you are about to read, in Jesus' name. Amen.

CHAPTER 1

What Do Mystical Experiences Feel Like?

God Keeps Trying to Communicate with Us

Christianity has a doctrine referred to as "God's ongoing self-revelation." This simply means that God wants us to constantly learn more and more about Him. I know that this is true from my own experiences, which this book is all about. Over human history, mankind had developed an increasingly accurate picture of God and the divine, spiritual realm. It also means that a person who devotes his or her life to God studies, meditates, and prays and will end up knowing more about God than the people who wrote the Bible. Oh boy! Is that sentence heretical? I don't think so, but some traditional literalists may. As a side note, I should reveal that I am what you could consider a liberal, out-of-the-theological-box thinker and lover of God. So, writing things like that does not bother me. Besides, all theological progress is born out of heresy anyway. Study the word *heresy*, and you will discover what I mean. Now that one will get the literalists really going. But remember Jesus Christ himself was accused of blasphemy, so thinkers like me are in the greatest of company.

Before I start to describe my personal mystical experiences, it is good to review divine encounters in general. To be sure, there are many in the Bible. Please read them in both the Old and New Testaments. There are many stories about divine encounters. St. Paul's encounter with the Risen Christ on the road to Damascus is a very good one. It can be found in the Book of Acts chapter 9, Saul's Conversion. St. Paul's original name was Saul until Jesus gave him the name Paul.

In Genesis, the encounter Moses had with God himself in the burning bush. This is an amazing account when God appeared to Moses within a burning bush. The fire did not consume the bush. God then gave him the commission to take the Hebrews out of Egypt. This can be found in the Book of Exodus chapter 3.

A last example would be when Mother Mary was told by an angel she would become pregnant with Jesus by the Holy Spirit. This can be found in the Gospel of Luke 1 26:38. These are three great examples of divine mystical experiences documented in the Bible. There are many more documented in the Bible. The point here is that divine mystical experiences have been going on since the Biblical times. I believe that they even occurred before then but documentation and what they called them serve to cloud these events.

These stories will serve as a foundation for a deeper understanding about the personal godly encounters I have experienced in my life. It will also serve to help you discern experiences you may have had in your life that may be of divine origin. Mystical experiences happen all the time. This is one way God talks to us in our lives today. Yes, I really do mean today! God is always trying to get our attention—if we would only shut off our damned iPhones, Xboxes, and TVs. There is nothing much good on anyway. The rest is plain junk with so much violence that most people think is entertainment. It is not entertainment. It is violence and nothing more. Yes, I am dating myself.

We all need divine guidance, and God uses many ways to get his personal message to us. My spiritual director likes to say that "God is closer to us than our own breath." I believe this is true, and God uses lots of ways to communicate with us. Mystical experiences are just one of those ways. Many people today believe that divine experiences are something of the Bible and do not occur in modern life. This is just not true. The events in my life serve as testimony that mystical events occur all the time. They occur today, right here and now, and to many people. They probably have happened in your life without your even realizing it. This is because God chooses to work in subtle ways, softly like the wings of a butterfly or the gentle rustling of leaves during autumn.

Other times, it is unmistakable that it is God bringing you an overwhelming divine experience. In my life, I have had the full range of mystical experiences from the ever-so-soft, yet elegant, flight of a hummingbird, the dramatic and intense appearance of divine spiritual beings, and being suddenly yanked out of my body and taken to the heavenly realm for a discussion with powerful divine beings to the magnificent sight in my wife's room of Jesus Himself when she was so very sick with cancer.

I believe most people do not recognize the spiritual when it happens around them. Most of the time, God works softly in love and peacefully in gentle whispers into our heart of hearts. Life is full of noisy clattering and banging that can drown out the beautiful songs and messages of God. And even if something spiritual happens and is taken note of, most people pass it off as being just one of those things. I pray that by reading this book, you can look back at your own life and recount when something out of the ordinary and unexplainable happened. It could have been the divine reaching out to you in order to help you in some way you did not expect. This, by the way, is one hallmark of a mystical experience. It comes unexpectedly. If you have a prayerful and open mind, the eyes to see, and the ears to hear, you will begin to see the divine spiritual world in action in a way pastoral ministers call mystical.

In my case, God has used a variety of ways to reach out to me. They have been partially through the mystical experiences that I document in this book. But there have been other ways God has used me too. My suggestion is to simply realize God is not limited to only a few ways to intervene in our lives and guide us in our actions and thoughts. It is just not the mystical as I will describe in this book. The kind of communications of our God in the Bible to many people in both the Old and New Testaments continue to this day. Communications from God could come in the form of a feeling that unexpectedly comes over you. It could be something a friend said that resonated instantly within you. It could be a stranger who says something to you that makes you wonder, "How did he know about that?" It could come while a song is playing on the radio and stirs your heart toward a peaceful contentment regarding a prayerful answer you were looking for. It could indeed be in a dream that plainly is meant to guide you regarding something.

There are so many different ways God communicates with us every day if we pay attention. A number of the mystical experiences I document here are ones that were unexpected and shocking in nature. They brought a quivering of my soul, a tingling of my heart and my skin. They are harbingers of love and hope guiding me down the path my spiritual journey must take according to God's divine will. They bring with them the divine power that can shake a person to the center of their being. The power of the divine mystical can be overwhelming or as soothing as the sweet song of a dove at dawn. But its source cannot be denied for it is from the hand of God himself. Of this, there can be no doubt. This has happened numerous times in my life, and I document some of them here for your own information and guidance.

Some of the other experiences I document in this book are like this. They involve the appearance of real spiritual beings and even unexpected and uninvited travel out of my body. It all depends on what was needed at the time. God continues to eagerly reveal himself to all His children who are willing to listen, see, and experience Him in their lives today. God indeed did not shut up two thousand years ago.

Experiencing the divine mystical also reveals the nature, personality, and loving characteristics of God our Father. We can learn much about God through these experiences. At the end of each section, I review what we can learn about God through each of the personal experiences I have documented. I have written about only those that I felt were significant and informational for the benefit of all those who take the time to read what I have written. I will not interpret my experiences but rather use them to reveal an increased understanding of God through them as best I can. I feel very humbled to have had so many mystical experiences. I know that part of the reason I have had them was to communicate them to others so all can understand God more deeply and be drawn closer to God.

These stories I will tell you may challenge your preconceived notion of the universal order of things. They may challenge certain parts of religious doctrines that are well-established within our society. They may challenge many people's belief systems that they cling to. They may challenge certain parts of your own belief system. Yet everything that has happened to me is consistent with loving and open Christian thought. As you read this, please have an open mind, open eyes, open ears, and open heart to what God is telling you through my experiences. In some way or another, each of us represents an image of God. This book represents some of the things that I believe God wants many of His children to understand about the nature of creation and of Himself and His only begotten Son, Jesus Christ. In one of my experiences, Jesus did appear. It occurred in a very intense moment in my life. What a wonderful and overwhelming event that was. I will detail this later.

The Characteristics of Real Divine Experiences

These qualities of different mystical experiences I learned by what I have directly experienced. Everything in this book is what has happened to me personally, as well as the circumstances that surrounded the divine events in my life. So what are the characteristics of a genuine mystical experience?

In no particular order, the first of the qualities is that there is an inability to really accurately describe the experience using normal

English words. Somehow, mystical events just go beyond a person's ability to relate in words what happened. In theological terms, this is called *ineffability*. It is so hard to put into words what it is like to have a divine mystical experience.

A writer like me fails to completely describe the feelings and content of a mystical experience. Words are just not enough to convey the nature of these experiences. They go well beyond our primitive language. There is indeed a poverty of words involved where nothing can truly describe these events. God and the unseen part of creation are beyond what can be told with mere words. Over the eons, language has been developed to deal with the physical world and human emotions but not the spiritual world. With this in mind, I will do what I can to paint accurate images and the feelings I experienced of the mystical with the brush of English words to describe what it is like to have divine mystical events as we travel together through the pages of this book.

Mystical experiences can be so strong and mind-blowing that there is no question that God created it. They can capture every sense of your body and occupy your entire mind for the time they manifest themselves. For me, my very first mystical experience was like this. It was so very powerful that I never imagined something could exist like that.

Others can be like a gentle caress of a whispering breeze, ever so soft to the touch as if they were on gossamer wings. They may bring a warmness and contentment to your soul. These too can be discerned as true and divine as has happened also to me many times.

These kind of experiences are especially common when I give Reiki sessions to my clients. The most wondrous tingling sensation permeates my entire body. They come in three waves, starting at my head and then enveloping my entire body. I can tell you without any doubt that these sensations are the most pleasurable feelings that I have ever experienced in my entire life. When they occur, I so desperately want them to never end.

The second quality of a mystical experience is that it may reveal to you some information that you could never know any other way. The information would otherwise not be available to you or would be hidden in some manner. In theological terms, this is called a noetic quality. In the simplest form, this would be new information about something that just comes to you. Perhaps later you will find out that it is very true. Plato used this term to describe the depths of the inner mind revealing truths to the conscious mind. Now, let's fast forward to Apollo 14 astronaut Edgar Mitchell. He had an epiphany after walking on the moon. He said that he felt the presence of divinity very strongly to the point that he just knew that life in this universe could never be just an accident based on random processes (think evolution). He felt a universal connectedness of all things. He said that this knowledge came to him directly. As a further comment, Edgar Mitchell later launched the interdisciplinary field of noetic sciences. His mystical experience inside the Apollo command module returning from the moon changed his entire life. And so it is with mystical experiences. They have the power to change lives. It did for me. For this, I am deeply grateful to our creator, God our Father.

The third quality or characteristic of a mystical experience is that it lasts a relatively short time. For me, these experiences are all too short and fleeting, yet they change lives for the better in every instance. Why? Because they come from God or are allowed by God to bring us closer to Him and to learn how to love Him in deeper ways.

It has been my experience that although the mystical lasts for a short time, during the experience, you lose track of normal time. You become unaware of the physical world that surrounds you. If your eyes are open, you will cease to see what it is you were looking at. You will cease to hear sounds. The feeling of sitting in the chair will go away; likewise with taste and smell. Your senses will seem as though they no longer function.

For the relatively short time a mystical experience is occurring, your entire being is involved and shuts out all other physical aspects of your existence. You become completely wrapped inside this godly experience that completely embraces your entire existence until its completion and then gently lets you go back into the physical realm, forever changed and closer to God. Each time this has happened to me, I did not want the mystical experience to end. I did not want to return to my so-called normal physical life. But the inevitable occurs and retuning to this physical world always brings with it a major letdown and feelings of wanting to return to live the mystical again and again.

The fourth characteristic of a divine mystical experience is that no matter how long it has been since the experience occurred, you retain all the details of what happened in your mind. A mystical experience is retained in your memory with much greater clarity and for a far longer time than normal events. This may be due to a number of things: the shock value of it, the great intensity of it, your emotions at the time it happened, or the great relief it may bring during a very stressful time in your life. It could also be a mystical mechanism that involves our inner being that works without us understanding it. No matter how this works, it is a great blessing from God that we retain the detailed memory of divine interaction with us very clearly to remind us that God is always with us. I want to emphasize this point. Mystical experiences are always happening to many people all over the world. This is proof that God is always with us every second of our physical existence.

I am a person who does not remember what I had for lunch yesterday. However, I remember with exact detailed clarity my first real mystical experience forty-five years ago. I remember everything. The next chapter describes all this and all that happened. Another reason I believe mystical experiences are remembered so vividly is that when God speaks, we listen with our complete inner being. This is such a wonderful thing. We all carry within the deepest part of our souls a spark of the divine, and I believe from my own experiences that it is the mystical events that awaken this divine spark. It carries on within us to guide and allow us so very clearly what God has said to us in our mystical experiences. We never forget, never at all.

The fifth quality of the mystical is that it comes unexpectedly. You cannot conjure them up at will. A mystical experience usually does not happen during mediation or prayer. Sometimes it does, though, as I have personally experienced. Meditation is always a good thing to do. It sets the stage for a mystical event. However, it is not necessary that something mystical will always follow. On the other hand, I have also had some divine experiences occur at stoplights. My mind seems to go blank waiting for the light to change, and this appears to create an opening for something that God wishes to tell me. In my case, the knowledge imparted to me during these short times at stoplights usually addresses a subject that has been on my mind recently.

Only God knows why this happens at such weird times, but this has occurred quite a number of times to me. These touches of the divine come according to God's time, not ours. They occur according to His will and not ours. When they do come, feel very blessed and humble that you have been in direct communication with the divine spiritual world. When they have happened to me, it always has left me with a feeling of intense peace in my heart. My body will tingle, and I feel like God was telling me, "Remember, Rich: I am always with you."

The sixth characteristic is that mystical events usually contain some sort of information that you did not expect. When this happens, you can rule out your imagination. Many times, people who have not had mystical experiences think that they are a product of human imagination. But a true mystical experience comes from not the imagination but God or sometimes another divine being in the spirit world, like an angel. They will bring with them a message containing information that was not previously known. This rules out the imagination. There is nothing in our imaginations that can surprise us. Mystical experiences will shock you at times as they have me.

The seventh characteristic of the mystical is that they are almost always voiceless. I do not hear English words but rather a telepathic knowing that comes instantly. A lot of new information that would take some time to describe in words can be understood in an instant during a mystical event. This kind of thing has happened to me a number of times. This is another way to know if something is from

God or not. There are times, however, when an angel may appear. This is what happened to me as part of my first mystical experience. An angel appeared as a normal-looking human being. More on that in the next chapter.

Most of the time, divine mystical experiences will bring with them a deep inner sense of peace and serenity. But in a few instances, this was not the case. It is like the time when the doctor found my wife's tumor, and I instantly saw a road ahead of us. It looked like it was a very long and painful one, ending in blackness. I saw this with my spiritual eyes, and it ran chills down my spine, as well as an overwhelming sense of dread and foreboding. I knew exactly what was ahead, and I was absolutely terrified. Everything around me in that hospital ward became completely blocked, and I went to another painful place where everything became very clear about what was going to happen in the coming years with my dear wife. God was preparing me for an awful and painful journey that both of us had to take together as a married couple. Oh, how painful was the road I saw us having to take to its final conclusion of death for my wife. All this occurred within very few seconds of the doctor telling me he found the tumor. But God was showing me what I needed to be prepared for. It was coming our way. A freight train loaded with agony and suffering was coming our way. There was no way to avoid it. All I could do was to prepare as best I could. I certainly did not expect this to happen.

Information given during a mystical experience is generally not spoken. You will not hear anything in the normal way. You will not hear a voice. Rather, it is silent and given in a telepathic way. God speaks silently. Yes, I said *silently*. Knowledge is imparted to you in a way that knowing takes place. This knowing may be communicated in the form of an image, like the road I just discussed. It may be an intense feeling or other ways that God knows you will respond to. These happenings are also testimony and proof that our true nature as beings is that we are not physical in our true essence. Rather, we really are eternal spiritual beings just having a human physical experience.

A mystical experience may be a communication to you that urges you to make a decision in a certain way. Or it may contain a warning. I had one of these kinds of experiences just the year before I wrote this book. You can always tell if it is a legitimate mystical experience by looking back after a period of time and seeing what would have happened if you had chosen against what the mystical experience urged you to do. In my case, I chose against what I was told. It would have been disastrous for my life. Sometimes, I can be a hardhead. I was told several times not to do something I was planning. I did anyway, and things went sour very quickly. I learned my lesson and got back on track. I will explain this later in more detail.

The eighth characteristic is something that does not happen very often. But when it does, it is a very powerful experience. It is something that you will remember your whole life. For reasons unknown to me, God decided to allow me to visit a little bit of heaven. This happened multiple times. I learned about a small portion of heaven and was amazed at what I found there. My wife, who died several years earlier, accompanied me, pointing out various things of interest. I explain the details these visits later in this book, as well. This is an out-of-body experience kind of experience. I had another out-of-body experience while on a cruise ship—more about that later, as well.

The ninth characteristic of mystical experiences is that they involves your body's physical and emotional reaction to them. Real mystical experiences can produce strong sensations while the imagination never does. Right after my first mystical experience on the jet, I was so overwhelmed with the intensity of the love that I felt that I began crying with joy and gratitude. Other mystical experiences have given me very strong and intensely joyful and pleasurable tingling sensations throughout my entire body as well. The joys of the tingling sensations are so pleasurable that I wished they would never end. It has been for me the most wonderful experience I have ever had in my life.

The tenth characteristic of mystical experiences is that they are effortless in that you do not have to do anything; you do not have to work at it. They just happen on their own, and you react to their actions. It is not like imagination, where you have to work at producing a thought or a feeling. Mystical experiences occur with their own energy, and you become largely a passive receiver. This accounts for the vast majority of mystical experiences that I have had.

The eleventh characteristic of some mystical events is where the recipient can become an active participant where it involves actual interactive communications between me and other divine spirit beings. This was the case when I was literally summoned out of my body to be in the presence of two very powerful divine spirits who wanted to hear what I had to say about my wife's sickness. In this case, I spoke to them, and they reacted to what I had to say before sending me back into my body. Another time I had a frank discussion with God our Father Himself. What an experience that was. I have also written about these experiences in detail in the following pages. These particular experiences contained all the primary characteristics of something divine—something real and something very mystical.

The twelfth characteristic of mystical experiences is really something that I find completely wondrous. The phenomenon is that the person receiving the mystical experience can see the spiritual being involved but NOBODY else can. This is what happened to me during my very first mystical experience. I had a very intense event. The complete story is described in later in this chapter. I could see a spiritual being in the airplane that told me telepathically that "God loves you." It was overwhelming in its simplicity and absolute divine power. This characteristic is that in this airplane there were other people close to me, but I was the only one to see this spiritual being.

This same thing happened to Marilyn as she was in the initial stages of dying from her cancer. While she was in the hospital, she asked me if I could see two men sitting next to the door. I could not, but she could see them clearly. More on this event in a later chapter. The idea here is that only the selected person intended to receive a mystical experience will see other beings while a person standing next to the recipient will not see or hear a thing.

This final comment is more of an observation and not a characteristic. From all the mystical events I have experienced, I have come to understand that the divine spiritual realm knows where we are every second of our lives. The being that came to me in the middle of the Pacific Ocean at 35,000 feet knew exactly where I was. This is the only way my experience could have happened.

I also got the feeling during the mystical experience that time and distance did not matter to this divine being. It was as if no matter where I was in the world, distance did not matter at all to this being. It was almost as if I felt I was traveling fast, but to this divine being, I was perceived to be stationary. This is very weird, but we all need to open our minds very wide to begin to understand the vast difference in physical laws here in the material world and how different they are in the heavenly realm. Later in this book, I go into much detail about this.

Summary

Usually, people think of mystical experiences as one-time events that occur and then go away. It's more like something strange happened, but it will never happen again, and people don't want to deal with the truth of it all. But I need to point out that the spirit world is available to us all the time. Some people are gifted to one degree or another where they have an ongoing awareness of the spirit world and the beings that inhabit it. This also includes seeing and hearing divine spiritual beings during the normal course of a person's life. As for me, God has blessed me with the gift of sometimes being able to see and hear some spirit beings at certain times. It is limited, but this includes my wife who passed away. There are multiple stories about this later in the book, but my experiences are not limited to just one person who has gone to heaven. There are others, including angels.

For me, I tend to get subtle or gentle mystical experiences at random times during some days. For me, at least, they tend to happen during my regular days with nothing special going on. I may be doing something, and then much like a person entering the room, a spirit being catches my attention. Usually, nothing is said or communicated.

But the message to me is, "Don't worry. I am here to support and love you." There are times when I can see the general features of the spirit, but not always. On the other hand, when my deceased wife wants my attention, I can see what she is wearing and what she looks like.

Finally, we need to remember that all this occurs within God's divine creation that has been lovingly designed for us and His other children so we may grow closer toward Him and fulfill our potentials determined at the beginning. Creation is not only the physical material that we see every day. The essence of creation is consciousness and that forms a divine matrix of loving and intermingling kindred spirits. This matrix extends across both sides of the veil and connects the physical world with the spiritual world. It is love that freely flows across or through the veil. It is love that allows communication from the physical world to the spiritual world and vice versa.

Do not restrict yourself to believing that "God is in heaven, and I am here." Do not think that spiritual divine events occur only to so-called gurus or monks. No! The divine spirit world overlays this physical world. God is eager to reveal it to us. The veil that separates the seen from the unseen is getting thinner and thinner. You can access the divine through prayer to God our Father and ask him to give you the grace and blessings of becoming aware of the divine unseen. Do not force it, but pray this way with your heart and peacefully lie back and discern how God answers your prayer. He will let you know. You may get a loving visit from Jesus Christ. Who knows?

God does not reserve the divine just for a special few. I believe that having mystical experiences is intended to be a normal part of human life. You do not have to be a guru or be especially gifted to have God interact directly with you. God loves all his children equally and shows no favorites. If a person puts God first in his or her life, loves others as himself, has an open mind and heart, and prays regularly, doing these things will open the door. God will be happy to walk through. Jesus Christ will walk through the door into your heart and begin guiding you in a holy life of love and peace that knows no limits. It is then that divine spiritual experiences are able to happen according to one's needs or the needs of other people in someone's life. Remember that God so loves the world that he gave His only begotten Son so that whoever believes in Him will not perish but have everlasting life. If God was willing to do that, why would he not also provide the mysterious divine experiences to all of us that lead us to him and the kingdom?

Many people can have a mystical experience and not understand what happened and shrug it off as just one of those things. I think this happens to a lot of people. Go back through your life and think of the times where something happened that you wondered about. It could have been a true mystical experience from the divine. Maybe not, but then again, maybe so. There is a saying that goes as follows: "Always be kind to strangers for sometimes you may be entertaining angels."

Was That from God?

You probably have never been taught about this, but you can tell if something is from God or not. Some people say that we are all being fooled by the devil as he can appear as an angel of light. Although this can be true and we all must be diligent and careful, there are some ways to test if something is from God or not. Also, our own emotions can sometimes seem like they are from the divine. Maybe they are. But the vast number of our experiences is just from daily life and not initiated by the divine. There are times when I cannot be sure if something is from God or my noisy brain. There have been many times in which I have an important question or issue that is facing me, and I have prayed for an answer. While doing something else, a thought breaks into my consciousness that addresses that issue. Well, I am left to wonder if it came from God or if it was my unconscious speaking out.

This is where careful discernment comes into play. Each of us must determine if good will come out of what has come to our conscious and if it does feel, and I mean really and objectively feel, like it was from God or another source. Yes, the waters do many times get muddy, but with prayerful consideration, we can sort things out for the benefit of not only ourselves but others, as well. And that is the primary question you must ask yourself in your discernment. Who will benefit if I take the course of action that has come to me? So we must be careful not to think everything comes from God. Usually, it is just part of our noisy brains and physical life itself. But be aware that something that comes to you could indeed be directly from God. Don't miss that!

One of my most powerful mystical experiences was definitely *not* from the divine. Rather, it was from hell itself. It was one of the most awful experiences I have had in my life. I will describe that later in this book. But there are a number of ways that generally guide us to know if something is from God or not. The following is not an exhaustive list, but it will give you an idea of the kind of things to look for.

One way is to simply pray to God our Father and God our Mother and ask them if this is from you. This is obvious once you think about it. Does the experience give you peace in your heart? It will if it is from God. There should be a peaceful inner knowing that the answer you received is from the divine. Also ask yourself if this experience is consistent with the Ten Commandments and biblical teaching. It will if it is from God. You can also take your story of your experience to someone with true Christian spiritual authority. Discuss it with them.

There are other ways to discern if something is from God or not. See what path the experience leads you toward. Is it a path of love for yourself and others and enlightenment? It will be if it is from God. Does the mystical experience leave you with peace in your heart? It will if it is from God. Does the experience prepare you for something in the future that you will need to know? It will if it is from God. Does the experience call you to some kind of action that will result in benefiting another person? It will if it is from God. Can you sense a deep and abiding love within the mystical experience, no matter what form it may take? You will if it is from God. Does it open your heart wider to be more loving and accepting of other people? It will if it is from God. Does a mystical event ring true in your heart and mind? It will if it is from God. If you are unsure, seek out other knowledgeable

Christians and discuss it with them. If a mystical event occurred a long time ago, do you remember it clearly with all the details? If it is from God, you will. Will good come from what you have received from the divine? It will if it is from God.

Mystical experiences are for our spiritual benefit and the conduct of our lives on this planet. They are inexorably intertwined with the ebb and flow of the events in our personal lives. They can occur to help you weather the rough seas of life, teaching you that God is always with you. From these kinds of thoughts, I believe you can get the idea of the general characteristics of a mystical experience and whether it is from God. Lastly, please remember that our God is a loving God of truth. You can rely on any and all divine mystical events in your life for they reveal truth about whatever is happening in your life.

We all need to remember that God is fully involved today with his ongoing revelation of himself to those of us with open minds and open, loving hearts. Thus, we do know much more today about God, His divine character, and His will and sacred personality than we did when the Bible was written. The divine mystical experiences that I write about are small ways that fit in with His plan to reveal His own majesty and infinite wisdom and existence to His beloved children.

I want to mention that God also intervenes in our lives behind the scenes. He works through bringing together circumstances that bring about his will for our benefit. This kind of godly action is not what I would label as mystical, but nonetheless, it is godly in its source. For example, I believe that God has been directly involved in my life, guiding me to make the right choices. There have been times when I chose wrong, and somehow, God would short-circuit the bad results that could have occurred. Our Lord, I believe, also has brought me together with people that I have deeply loved. He has indeed answered my prayers many times. I have also been blessed with the ability to sometimes see divine spirits and communicate with them. I have documented a few of these stories in this book.

I am greatly humbled that God chose me to become a spiritual writer. He has placed in my heart the desire to bring others of His children closer to Him through what I write. But He also knows that I remain not too thrilled in revealing what I do in this book. It is so very personal. But for the love and spiritual growth of His other children, I will do this for our Lord Father. I do pray that this book becomes a blessing for you and your spiritual life and brings you closer to God our Father.

Why Me?

I feel that in my case, the mystical experiences I have had (and continue to have) have a twofold purpose. The first is to keep me going in this physical life. I have had many traumatic events occur in my life and suffer from certain ailments that continue to haunt me every day, every hour, and every minute of my time on earth. God must have decided to support me in this life with these glimpses of the divine to remind me that there are many people who need me and I must stay in the physical realm to complete my assignment here.

The other reason I have mystical experiences is for the direct benefit of others of His children. Certain things have happened in my life that have allowed me to assist others in avoiding bad mistakes or help in other ways too. In this sense, I am a conduit for God to reach some of His children to help them. Many times, I have felt that I am an emissary of God's love to certain people I have come in contact with. It is a teaching role to those who very much needed it. After my assignment is complete, I will move on. There was one person who thought what I just said was bizarre. All that shows is that the person who said it has a long way to go on her spiritual journey.

It is because of God's love extending into the physical world that prayers are heard. Our prayers do indeed penetrate the veil and are always heard by God. It is my personal belief that it is impossible for God not to hear every prayer that is ever said. Creation is a masterpiece of divine intellect, and you and I are an inexorable part of that. The characteristics of mystical experiences I have just discussed only scratch the surface of how inexorably intertwined and connected together the seen physical world and the unseen spiritual world are. I know what I have said is true because everything I just discussed I have personally experienced. I write only about those things that I have experienced. It is in this way that I ensure that every word I write is true and complete. May God bless you and enrich your lives through the words I write. That is my desire. That is my prayer.

Now let's start with the stories of my mystical life.

CHAPTER 2

My Mystical Life Begins

My First Mystical Experiences

*I*t was an absolutely beautiful day in Honolulu. The sun was shining. Gentle balmy breezes were flowing and gorgeous, and beautiful puffy clouds were scattered about the sky. As they say, it was another day in paradise. I was walking down the sidewalk where all the large hotels are and enjoying the sights and sounds I had never seen before. For the first time since I was married, I was by myself. My family had gone on to the Philippines to visit other family members a few days prior. I stayed behind because I had always wanted to explore Hawaii. This was my chance. My wife and I liked Hawaii so much we were considering moving there. She was Filipina, and I am Croatian, so I thought she would perhaps feel more comfortable with the larger Asian population if we lived there. But we decided not to since job opportunities were far better in Silicon Valley where we met.

I was about twenty-six years old when this story took place. During this time in my life, religion or spirituality or anything to do with faith never really entered my mind. I was still carrying within me the disdain and intense dislike of the Catholic Church from my four years at St. Tarcissus in Chicago, Illinois. It was run by cruel German nuns who made the school into something of a detention camp. The slightest infraction of any of the myriad of rules had immediate results by big bellowing nuns in gigantic black habits descending upon you. To me, they looked like elephants thundering toward you. I think this school with these nuns is where the term *thunder thighs* got started. They would have horribly angry expressions on their faces and waddle down the hallways like sumo wrestlers with their thighs slapping together.

Fear was the order of the day at that school. This was only nine years after the end of WWII. Perhaps these sumo nuns were pissed off at losing the war and were getting even with the kids of the generation that had kicked their asses in Germany. Who knows? Okay, yes: I just went over the edge, but that was the way it was. This was really my only direct exposure to the Catholic Church, so-called faith, spirituality, and God. I didn't like one bit of it. Religion and "God stuff" was like taking castor oil for me. All of it was bitter and did no good at all; it was a complete waste of time and full of pain.

Up until this point, when this story takes place, I don't think I ever used the word *God* if it weren't followed by the word *dammit*. Little did I know what was in store for me over the next few days. God had his plan for me, and I had absolutely no idea what was coming my direction. Yes, one of the defining characteristics of a true mystical experience is that it is unexpected. Boy, my first one sure was. I was to find out that God has plans for all of us no matter what level of faith or lack of faith we may have at the time. God will never abandon us and His love for us is indeed unconditional regardless of our bad attitude toward faith, spirituality, and him for that matter. I should know. I was one of those who thought I was beyond religion and all the crap that it entailed. I was thankfully very wrong. Thankfully, God had more faith in me than I did in him.

In my life up to this point, I never even heard of mystical experiences, much less having experienced one myself. I don't think I ever heard the word *mystical*. As a small kid, I was taught that priest had to intercede for us with God so our little sinful hinnies would not roast in the eternal barbeque along with Satan and his buddies. We were all told many times that we were all deserving of hell, and only going to Mass every Sunday, obeying the Catholic Church, and following *all* the rules might just get us out of the eternal furnace. Talk about instilling fear into little susceptible minds! We were taught the fear of God, not the love for God. Knowing what I know now, I wonder how many of those priests and nuns at St. Tarcissus did not go to heaven but instead sadly went to the hell they preached at us about. I wonder.

An Angel on the Street

Have you ever had an experience with another person that you did not know that seemed weird at the time? Perhaps it was if that person knew you somehow, but you did not know him. Or perhaps he said something to you that struck you and you did not know how to respond. This is how my first real-life mystical experience started. I was walking down the street in Honolulu. As I walked down that sidewalk, something was going to start to happen that would change my bad attitude about things spiritual very quickly. I would come to realize that angels were there even for me. It became a life-changing event that would go unnoticed by everyone around me on that street that afternoon.

As I walked along the sidewalk, I saw a man up ahead of no particular description, and across the street from this man, there were three or four people who had their heads shaved except for a very long topknot of hair. They were dancing and clicking finger cymbals together, obviously performing a religious ceremony of some sort. What they were doing interested me, and I was looking at them while I was walking. I was looking at these dancing men as I walked closer to this man standing ahead of me. There were other people coming and going just as you would expect in downtown Honolulu around dinnertime.

As I got closer to this man, I noticed he was looking at me. Why,

I did not know. I was just one of many people passing by. It made me feel uncomfortable. But as strange as it may seem, it was as if he knew what I was thinking about those dancers across the street. He approached me and said without any hesitation as I got within speaking distance of him, "That is not the way." I stopped and looked at him with a surprised expression on my face. How did he know what I was thinking? I felt like I was somehow compromised where my internal thought have been invaded. He went on to say that he was with a Christian group and that they were going to have a meeting in the park that was close by in a couple of days. He handed me a small flyer. I thanked him for the flyer and told him that I would be leaving for the mainland the next day and couldn't attend the meeting in the park. The truth be told, I lied to him because I just didn't want to go to any stupid Christian meeting. And with that I began to walk away. I felt that something very weird just happened and wanted to just get away from this guy.

But then I felt immediately that something had just happened that was not of the ordinary. What it was, I had no idea. I got about ten steps away or so from this man, and something told me to look back at him. I expected to see him handing out flyers to other people walking on the sidewalk. That I did not see at all. Somehow, he had completely vanished. He was absolutely nowhere to be seen. He could not, under any circumstances, have walked away from where he was standing without me somehow seeing him since it was such a short distance that I had walked before I turned around. He was standing in an open area near a stop light, and there were no nearby places that he could have walked to that would have hid him from my sight.

That man just plainly vanished into thin air in the five to ten seconds since I spoke with him. Obviously, I have never forgotten that little thirty-second event in my life. How could someone I was just talking to vanish into thin air? At the time, I was perplexed. I could not understand how all this happened. It bothered me quite a bit. All that happened so quickly, and I just registered in my mind that it was just one of those things. I tried to dismiss it as inconsequential. But later I was to realize it really was not. It was something far beyond that. It was something that I never experienced before. It was something divine.

I have a dear friend—a Jesuit—who had a similar experience. Years later, he was standing in line to be seated at a restaurant with another friend. I was not there, but it is a restaurant that I went to frequently with him. As he stood in line with another friend to be seated, there was a model of the Hindenburg above their heads. His friend commented about what a tragedy that was. Then a man standing two feet behind them in line said, "I was there." They both looked at this man. He had a very sad expression on his face. He was very old-looking, with many wrinkles on his face. He had an air of desperation about him, and his clothes were of someone who was poor. Then my friend turned away from this man. Just a few seconds later, just a very few seconds, they both turned back toward that man. He had vanished completely. I know the long hallway patrons had to stand in to be seated. There was no way this man could have walked down the long hall that led to the check-in counter where my friend was standing. I know that restaurant, and it takes at least thirty seconds to walk down the hall to get to the check-in counter. But the man my friend and his companion were talking to just a few seconds prior had just vanished completely.

After consulting with several very spiritual people and priests, my friend was told by all of them that this man who disappeared was a person who didn't quite make it to heaven and was asking them for their prayers. He was the spirit of a man who had died and was allowed to appear in the physical realm to ask for help.

It was only after a few years that I realized the man I met on the street in Honolulu was an angel sent for my benefit to keep me on the proper spiritual path in light of my inner interest in what those tasseled dancers were doing across the street. It was a rare event to see grown men in gowns dancing on the street with finger cymbals and bald except for tasseled hair coming out of the top of their heads. After reviewing this event in my mind hundreds of times since then and growing in faith, I cannot help but reach the same conclusion over and over again. That man I encountered was indeed actually an angel who appeared like a normal human being. The angel was there specifically for my personal benefit to keep me on the proper path of faith that God, in His infinite wisdom, has planned for me. There can be no other reasonable explanation. Normal people just do not vanish. Only angels or other divine beings can do that. And yes, if you have any doubts, these things really did happen.

Divine Events

Have you ever had a wonderful feeling come over you? All of a sudden, the world looks far brighter and loving than it did just a few seconds prior, but no one around you has any awareness of what you are experiencing. It has always been interesting to me that divine events can occur with such a normal look and appearance about them. No one else walking on that sidewalk would have noticed anything out of the ordinary.

But a miraculous divine event was unfolding right there on that sidewalk in Honolulu among all the hustle and bustle of a busy city without anyone else noticing, just me. Divine events can appear in a normal setting, but they are not of this world. They are from our Heavenly Father who intervenes at precisely the right moments in our lives to keep us on track, to bring us peace, and to bring us consolation or whatever it is we may need at that moment in our lives.

These mystical events always appear so very normal to those not directly involved and can always be explained in secular physical terms if your mind is so inclined. If what happened to me and my friend also happened to an atheist or agnostic, they would just tell themselves that somehow the man they talked to just walked off and shrug it off. No more attention would be paid to the event. Their minds would immediately go on to something else because they are not open to God within themselves. But in my case, my mind was open to the spiritual and realized it was not normally possible since I could see all around.

It was impossible for the man in Honolulu to somehow get to a place that I could not see in the few seconds that had gone by before I looked back. Someone once said that we should always pay attention and be nice to strangers for we may be entertaining angels. I never realized how true that was until that day on the sidewalk so many years ago.

You can never explain away the physical and almost instantaneous disappearance of a human-looking being into thin air. This is what happened with that man on the street in Honolulu who gave me a small flyer for a Christian gathering. To this day, I now know and understand without any doubt that that man was an angel from God sent to protect me from straying off the spiritual path God wanted me to follow and to let me know that He is always with me, even though I cannot perceive Him with my five senses.

After describing this event, you would think that I would have either been all shaken up or on my knees in prayer to God. However, because of my mindset against the Catholic Church and religion in general at the time, neither of these things happened. At the time, it registered in my mind as merely a very curious event. It was an event that I would want to remember and someday talk about to other people who may have had similar experiences. But this was not an epiphany for me in any way, at least not at that time. The epiphany was only two days away and coming directly my way. I had no idea what was in store. However, I can say that I felt God was closer to me than He was before, and it heightened my sense of Christian morality and ethics. I did not know it at the time, but this event marked the beginning of my spiritual journey that continues to this day.

God's Little Test

We all have temptations, don't we? Little did I know that at the time, but this was just the first of three events that would occur in the next few days. The next evening, I was wandering around looking for a shirt to buy to commemorate my visit to Honolulu. I happened upon a small store and went inside. The very lovely Asian woman behind the counter waited on me, and we struck up a conversation. I picked out a shirt, and we continued talking. It became clear after a while that she was interested in me, even though I had told her I had been married for a couple of years. I let it slip where I was staying. She told me she got off at eleven and that perhaps we could have a drink. She said she could show me around the island the next day. I thought that would be a nice idea and said yes. I bought the shirt and left the store. I was so naive. Perhaps *stupid* might be a better word.

Then it hit me: *Just what kind of an idiot am I anyway?* I thought. I got very scared and didn't know what to do other than to never to see that girl again. Since I let it slip where I was staying and I knew she got off at eleven, I walked around Honolulu far from my hotel until about two in the morning. I didn't want to get anywhere near where she might be waiting for me. I couldn't help but think what an absolute moron I was and wanted no part of anything that might happen because of my stupidity. So when I thought the coast would be clear, I snuck up to my room, locked the door, and went to bed. Looking back, I can't help but feel that God was testing me with that very pretty Asian sales clerk.

Somehow, I knew that the man in the street who disappeared was there to renew my faith and that the pretty Asian woman was there to see if I was serious about my Christian values. I know that I had passed our Lord's test with flying colors. Nonetheless, I started to feel as though invisible forces had me in their sights. I felt uncomfortable and was wondering what was going to happen next. Well, I did not have to wait too long.

Divine Fireworks on the Flight Home

Then came the flight home. What happened next was something that hit me like a ton of bricks. It was life-changing to say the least. One of the characteristics of a real mystical experience is the unexpectedness and intensity of it. I would find out the next day just how unexpected and intense that could be.

There was nothing special about the first half of the flight. The excitement of the takeoff from Honolulu with its gorgeous scenery was breathtaking. The blue water of the Pacific was dazzling to the eye. My time in paradise had come to an end. I was sitting in the back on the left side of the airplane, enjoying the extra-large window and looking out at the Pacific Ocean below. I had absolutely nothing on my mind and was listening to the airplane's music system. The song "Go Your Own Way" by Fleetwood Mac was playing.

Then suddenly it happened! Oh, God, did it ever happen! What happened next would indeed begin to change my life like nothing else could. Unlike the man on the street, who was actually an angel, this experience is something that was so powerful, so unimaginably beautiful, and so penetrating straight to my heart that I could scarcely believe that it was really occurring.

Even to this day, this event remains so powerful in my mind that it indeed can still bring tears to my eyes. To say that it changed my life is an understatement. I can remember every little detail of what happened next.

The only way I can describe what happened is to use English words, but they will fail by their very primitive nature to describe the intensity, the utter level of love, the beauty, and the sense of God of the experience that I was about to have. Intellectuals call this phenomenon a *poverty of words*. Take what I am about to explain and multiply it by a thousand to get an idea of what I experienced.

Above me and a few feet forward to my right, a divine being appeared. Yes, a divine being appeared to me in that airplane high above the Pacific Ocean, about halfway from Hawaii to California. There was no mistaking what or who this loving being was or from where it came. I cannot describe to you what this being looked like other than to say I had a strong sense of this being as a three-dimensional spherical ball of pure lightly gold-colored energy that radiated enormous amounts of love, acceptance, compassion, and understanding. It was not a fixed sphere, but it was gently quivering with ripples that slowly moved around its surface. It was a conscious being for sure. I perceived that immediately. Even though I saw the sphere of golden light, it was quite ephemeral, translucent, and transparent. I could still see through it. I knew that I was the center of this being's complete attention. I knew that this being came into the airplane for me and only me. No one else on the plane stirred in the slightest. It was only me who could see this being floating above and to my right.

What I remember the most is the unfathomably intense amount of love that I felt this being directed toward me and into my heart. If you have ever in your life felt really loved, magnify that by a thousand to get an idea of the intensity of what I felt coming from this magnificently beautiful divine being. It was as if every cell in my body was being bathed in a pure divine elixir of love so intense that words completely fail to describe the love, beauty, and something of a shared existence I had with this being. Somehow my existence extended beyond this physical realm and into the realm where this intensely loving being came from. I have never felt that before or since. I could see this being had a certain shimmering quality about it. It was almost as if it were mildly pulsating with pure life that was unaffected by the moral dirt we all experience on this earth.

A few moments after its appearance, as I was experiencing this overwhelming love, this being said three words to me, and I heard them telepathically. I did not hear them with my ears. Instead, I heard these three words with my mind. This divine being was communicating with me telepathically, something I had never experienced before. This divine and loving being simply said the following words, "God loves you." It was said telepathically and without words. Somehow my brain understood it in words. This wonderful being only said this once. But that was all that was needed. After hearing this in my mind, my body began to tingle like I have never experienced before. It was the most pleasurable sensation I have ever felt. The deep soul-fulfilling warmth that I felt, the closeness to God that I felt, and the inner peace in my heart that I felt were so intense and so beautiful that I started to cry sitting there alone in my seat. I could have lived the rest of my life in that state of ecstasy. I really mean it when I say there is no love on this earth, no matter how wonderful it is, that comes anywhere near the overwhelming intensity of the love this divine being radiated into my inner being. Even to say that it was overwhelming understates the wonder of it all.

After this magnificent divine being told me, "God loves you," it stayed there suspended in the air of the aircraft cabin for a minute or two longer. But this time length I give you is only a very cursory estimate because as this was happening, I seemed to lose my sense of time, not altogether but close to it. For a while, it seemed that my only focus was this magnificent divine being that came to me with such an intense love and message for me. All I could do was stare at it and become completely immersed in the complete love it radiated toward me, a love that penetrated every cell in my body. In a sense, the two of us became one. By that I mean the connection between my heart of hearts and this divine being was so close that to say we became one for a moment would be valid. I have heard before that two could become one and now I have experienced it. It was an absolutely stunning and loving intense experience.

There were no other passengers around me who could see what was happening to me. But even if there were, I do not think that they could have in any way sensed what was happening. The light that came from this divine spirit should have been noticeable to some people a few rows up from me, but still nobody noticed anything. I sat there with tears flowing down my cheeks and experiencing such love and acceptance I never thought was possible.

After a few more moments, I felt like getting up from my seat and running up and down the aisle of the airplane, shouting at the top of my lungs, "God loves us, God loves us." But I didn't. I was still soaking in the ecstasy of the intense love being given to me by this divine being. With the tears flowing down my cheeks, I looked around the cabin. Everything appeared so very normal. The sounds of the engines were there, the air rushing past the airplane was there, and the music playing on the sound system was there, too. Here I was, having this completely unexpected intense spiritual and divine experience with this divine being only three or four feet away from me, yet everything else in the cabin looked completely normal and routine. This contrast between my intense experience and the dull routine of being in an airplane was absolutely shocking to me. Why weren't these other people reacting as I was? It seemed unfathomable to me, yet there it was before my very eyes.

Then a few moments later, this glorious and intense ecstasy of love and compassion that I was experiencing from this divine being began to slowly fade away. What returned to me were the sights and sounds of only this routine flight from Honolulu to San Francisco. To this day, I still ache to feel those sensations—love, compassion, and acceptance—again. It was an enormous experience that defies description. I hope the words I used to paint an image of this experience give you an idea of what happened that beautiful day high over the Pacific Ocean. I hope that you too can one day experience such unfathomable love one day in your life.

Looking Back at My Spiritual Beginning

These two mystical experiences and the test I had during the last two days of my vacation in Honolulu are what I look back as the beginning of my real Christian life—my real spiritual journey in this life. They were indeed complete life-changing turning points for me. Or as some people would say, an epiphany. These experiences changed my attitude toward religion and Christianity itself. It did not change my opinion of those cruel nuns back in Chicago, but my openness toward spirituality and faith in the Christian tradition had certainly changed in an enormous way. God saved me during those few days in Honolulu. For that, I am eternally grateful.

Being a pilot myself, I was fully aware of the altitude, speed, and direction of the aircraft. A question later came to me. How was it that the divine being knew where I was? How did it perfectly match the speed, altitude, and direction of that aircraft? How did the divine being know where I was sitting and my mental state at that time? All I know for sure is that the divine spirit certainly knew everything that day. I also have come to believe that God and His divine spirit beings know everything about us, know what we are doing, and where we are at every instant of our lives.

Frankly, that gives me great peace in my heart. The Bible says that God even knows how many hairs are on top of our heads. He knows us better than we know ourselves. I think you should believe that, for He certainly knew everything I was doing in Honolulu and found me on that high-flying jet coming home. Think about that. It is a magnificent comfort to know that God is so close to us that He or His messenger can appear to us in an instant, wherever we are and no matter what we are doing. God does love us unconditionally. He did this for me in spite of my negative attitude toward religion and the Catholic Church.

In the years after these experiences (and until now), I would experience many more and various levels and kinds of mystical experiences. I will share many of them with you in this book so you can also grow in faith, knowing that people do experience the divine directly even while on earth and not having any kind of near-death experience.

This is one thing I want to emphasize to you. Much has been made of near-death experiences over the past twenty years or so. People die clinically for a while and have similar experiences, seeing spirits or a white light and have various real experiences of heaven and sometimes hell. I think this is all fantastic. I believe this is all part of God wanting to continue his self-revelation to all His children. But I also believe that an unsaid assumption has crept into this field. That is, if you want to have spiritual experiences with the divine and heaven, you have to die and be revived in order to do it.

Well, that is not true. You do not have to almost die to directly experience the divine. I want to emphasize this. It is not in any way a requirement to almost die to directly experience divine love. I did by just flying in a jet over the Pacific Ocean and listening to music. I have had other heavenly spiritual experiences that I will discuss in a few chapters. I never came close to dying at any time. But I must also say that it is up to God's choosing the how and when if you experience what I have. Having these experiences or not also does not in any way serve as a report card on how good a Christian you may be or your chances of getting to heaven. God has His reasons for allowing my experiences, and to this day, I do not know the reason why. I have some strong ideas, but now is not the time to share them with anyone but my closest spiritual confidants.

What Did God Reveal of Himself?

What can we learn from the experiences I had during those two days? There are a number of things I think are good to remember in everyone's spiritual lives. Remember that God does things in our lives not only to teach us but also to reveal who He is and what He is like—in other words, His personality.

1. God does not discuss His plans for us before we start to experience them. He sent the angel on the street to me and the magnificent spirit being on the airplane without letting me in on His plans. In my prayer and meditation life, I never had God consult me before making things happen, which, by the way, always seems to work out just fine for me. There have been times when things seem dark with no way out. I pray for guidance and trust what the Bible says that all things work toward the good for those who love God our Father. But I do have to wait to see the good come out of things, and sometimes it seems just way too long. Well, most of the time, it seems that God always waits until the last minute before something good happens. I do not like waiting. Like my dear Jesuit friend always says, "Dear God, please give me patience, and I want it now!"

2. God knows what is going on inside our heads. Well, now that thought could be frightening to some people, but calm down.

He loves us no matter what is going on inside our cranium. Our thoughts are only our personal testing ground regarding possible actions. It is intentions and actions that count. So remember that no one is beyond His unconditional love. How else could He have sent that angel to tell me that the tasseled dancers were not the way? Yes, God knew what I was thinking and did something about it. He sent that angel to talk with me and then promptly disappear.

3. God seems to have more faith in us than we do in him. My level of faith was awful when all this occurred in Honolulu and the flight home, but these mystical experiences happened anyway and very much for my personal benefit. You do not need to be a priest, rabbi, monk, or guru for a mystical experience to happen to you. I am living proof of that.

4. God knows precisely where we are and what we are doing all the time. Otherwise, how could He send His angel to me on the street in Honolulu and the divine being to me in that airplane high above the Pacific Ocean? God must be all around us all the time. I discuss this in detail in another book I wrote "A Real Life Christian Spiritual Journey". This is really quite a wonderful thought, don't you think?

5. Space and time are not what they appear to us. Having a scientific background, I continue to be amazed that the divine being with me on the airplane was exactly matching the speed, direction, and height of the airplane. Somehow, I get the feeling that the heavenly realm that this divine being came from has different physical laws than we do in our physical reality. This has to apply to the humanlike angel, as well. The fact that the heavenly realm has different physical laws than we do was confirmed years later to me after my darling wife died. I will describe them later in this book. You will be amazed. I was.

6. There are most certainly other godly realms that we cannot normally perceive. The angel and divine being I encountered

had to come from somewhere else and go back there to a realm that we cannot see. This has to be. Also, we are separated from this higher realm by a veil that prevents us from seeing the other realm. But I can also say there is one thing that penetrates this veil with ease. That one thing is love. Further on in this book, you will see why I say this. I also have to say that there are limited times when I get a glimpse of spirit beings on the other side of the heavenly veil. Experiencing that makes it somewhat harder to remain in this physical realm, but I do for the love of our Lord Father and His plan for all of us.

7. God's love for us goes way beyond anything we can describe. Words fail completely to describe the intensity, purity, and overwhelming unconditional love He has for us as I felt it in that airplane. This is part of Christian dogma, and it is ever so true. I give you my testimony that this is completely true.

8. Be kind to strangers for you may be entertaining and be in the presence of angels. I was on the street in Honolulu. You may have likewise been in the presence of angels and not known it. Think about that. There are times that I wonder just how many angels there on earth with mankind doing the kinds of things the angel on the street in Honolulu did for me. The number I came up with is quite large. For me, this is a reassuring thought.

9. God did create different life forms in his creation. Angels, for example, are real, but do not have the restrictions of a physical body. They are spirits, for lack of a better word. Now if God is infinite as Christian dogma states, there are also no restrictions on God's capability to create all sorts of different kinds of living sentient beings in different realms. Admittedly, this is out of the theological box of thinking, but if we apply this reasoning to beings in the physical realm, this opens up the possibility that God may have chosen to also create other kinds of living sentient beings besides us humans. I do not know one way or another, but I imagine the possibility does exist.

CHAPTER 3

Long-Term Divine Mystical Guidance

Little Did I Realize What God Was Doing as It Happened

In the course of everyone's life, we all have had experiences that seem to be random and unconnected. Have you ever had a series of experiences over a long period of time where each of them seems to have no apparent connection among the others at the time? Yet, after a while, they all seem to come together in a way that makes something happen that never before seemed to possible.

It has been my experience that most people live from day to day and never look back at preceding events so as to connect the dots between them, learn how they were really part of a larger unfolding picture, and learn why the ending event took place that turned out better than it would have otherwise. I have always counseled people to look back at their lives, because it is in the looking back that you can see the fingerprints of God throughout your entire life, guiding you, loving you, and giving you certain feelings and urgings to do one thing versus another. All this is designed to make your future better if you are smart enough to follow God's urgings and guidance.

There is a classic story about a man who led a troubled life. He believed in God and thought that if he did believe, life would be better in the here and now. He went to church, was a good father and husband, and did what he could to help others. But during his life, he suffered a lot. In his mind, he could not reconcile why God would allow suffering for someone who believed in Him. This troubled the man immensely throughout his entire life. He asked himself why God would allow suffering of his children. Then the day came when this man passed away, and he went to heaven. He encountered our Lord Jesus Christ and asked Him the following question, "Why is it you allowed so much suffering in my life when I dedicated my life to you?" Jesus showed him his life as a series of footsteps in the sand. Jesus said that He accompanied him every step of the way throughout his life, the good times and the bad. Then the man saw two sets of footprints in the sand. But looking back at the footsteps, the man noticed that during the most difficult and painful times of his life, there was only one set of prints in the sand. The man became very disheartened and asked Jesus why He had abandoned him during the most difficult times of his life. Jesus said, "My dear son, it was during those times that I carried you." Those footprints were Jesus'.

My Mystical Dots

Before I tell a story of my life, I invite you to take a moment and think of something important that occurred in your life. Then, look at the preceding events and connect the dots. I bet you will find that the preceding events were indeed related, leading up to the final important event. Although sometimes you can detect a trend through reason, logic, and intuition, most of the time, connecting the dots can be a difficult thing. But if you can connect the dots, then you just may learn something very important about God and His participation in your life.

The Story

In the following story starts after I left NASA and went to work for Hewlett Packard. There were lots of mystical dots, and I did not have a clue what God was preparing me for. During this time in my life I had many mystical urgings to follow a certain path, starting in my midtwenties. It was only when I was in my midfifties that I was in a position to look back and connect all the many dots that led up to a serious, life-changing event. So this story is about thirty years of God's guidance so that we could survive as a family. At the time the various events or dots were happening, I did not understand they were parts of a much larger pattern that led to a terrible life-changing event headed our way. I had absolutely no idea.

What happened took a little more than thirty years for the series of both normal and mystical events to unfold to its climax. There are times when a divine plan for your life takes a series of mystical experiences, various events, and divine urgings over a very long time to come to completion. As each little apparently unrelated divine event occurs, it seems like nothing important. Yet each one is part of a much larger puzzle that we cannot see at the time, but God does. When the puzzle of little divine urgings and mystical events is complete, you are now prepared to deal with a large significant and life-changing event to occur. At the time each piece of the puzzle occurs, it is very hard or impossible to detect why these things are happening. In my case, I had no clue where all this was leading.

After I got back from my vacation in Honolulu, life went on in a very normal way. My wife, our little girl, and I were happily living in a townhome we bought. I was starting my career in computer marketing with Hewlett-Packard, and I would bicycle to work every day since we only had one car. It was a big-ass Chrysler that we affectionately called The Tank. My wife was learning how to drive in it.

What changed in this preparation was my increased openness to God and living my life in a more God-centered way. I knew that God sent that divine being to me in the airplane over the Pacific Ocean to open my heart so I could now be sensitive to and hear God's divine guidance and urgings about what I had to do in the coming years. The urgings I received from God were to get involved in real estate. I kept getting these urgings as this was the way for the future for me and my family. In response to these urgings, I got my real estate salesman license and later my California Real Estate Broker's license too.

The townhome development we were living in was far from complete, and I got motivated to get a second job on Sundays as a salesman in the sales office, selling the very same kind of townhome we were living in at the time. My real estate license allowed me to work in the sales office and receive a small salary and commission for any units I sold. So at that time I had two jobs, one working for Hewlett-Packard and the other working for the real estate development company. During this time, we saved as much money as we could because we knew our family would grow and that we would need a larger home in the not-too-distant future.

Also during this time, I still did not have very many thoughts about God. However, there were some significant changes that were taking place within my inner being. I had become more open to the things of God and realized that God was more real than I had ever thought of before my experiences in Honolulu. I still did not go to church very much. I still could not stand the thought of Catholicism because I equated that with the cruelty of the nuns in my childhood. In fact, my attitude was that at the time when my oldest daughter was three, I still expected her to go to public school to save her from the ravages of the way in which I was treated in parochial school.

But I was indeed more open to God. I also began to feel that God was not the same thing as the Catholic Church. Somehow the door to my heart was opening. So I paid attention to God our Father and His urgings about real estate. After we investigated where we would send our daughter to school and to my own surprise, we sent her to our local Catholic elementary school. I never thought that would happen but I felt good about that.

At this time, being involved in real estate felt right and good for our future, even though I had a very good job in marketing at Hewlett-Packard. There were plenty of promotional opportunities, and my income was very good. With my income from Hewlett-Packard, we bought a three-bedroom house in San Jose to live in and kept our townhouse as a rental. So we were doing quite well with my job at Hewlett-Packard and my Sunday job with the development company. Even beyond these two jobs, I still had these notions, urgings, and thoughts to get even more involved with real estate. The result was that we bought two more townhouses as rentals over the next three years or so. My feelings somehow still did not make sense regarding accumulating all this real estate. But I knew that I had to get a much larger wealth over the coming years. I still did not understand why.

I really did not realize at the time just how mystical my urgings were in preparing me for a change in life to come years later. I did not yet have the tools, knowledge, or ability to recognize a mystical event occurring right smack-dab in the middle of my head while God was talking to me in his silent telepathic way. God was bugging me through constant feelings instilled inside me that I just had to be really successful both at Hewlett-Packard and real estate investing. Believe me, you do not want God bugging you and to not do something about it. God can be relentless. I bought and sold real estate as a broker for clients and invested in real estate for my family, and all the while, I had a full-time, pressure-filled career with Hewlett-Packard. I was a busy bee for many years.

More Is Revealed

After about six or seven years investing in real estate, I was given to know that my life would change greatly in my midfifties. Yes, I was told that a number of times in my quiet moments that my life would change a lot in my midfifties and that the money I was accumulating would be necessary for that time in my life. I never told anyone about these feelings and urgings. I kept it to myself. This knowledge about something in the future in my life came to me by way of deep feelings that would come in a second or two. No words ever were spoken. But I knew that this knowledge was not coming from me. No, it was coming from outside myself. Looking back, I now know it was from the divine spiritual realm, God himself. These multiple happenings carried much of the characteristics of a mystical experience, but these low-key urgings were over a period of time.

Nonetheless, it is appropriate to include this in my narrative. This was a time in my life where I was not nearly as attuned to God's sacred words as I am now. But I was spiritually attuned enough at this point that I could discern what would come from my own thoughts and what was coming from the divine and sacred spirit world. These silent urgings and knowledge were definitely coming from the spirit world. There was no doubt.

When these urgings would happen, I would just be given this knowledge in a flash. I would be thinking about something, my mind might pause for a moment, and then these flashes of urgings would happen. These things happened a number of times over the course of weeks. It was like God was repeating Himself so He was sure that I got the message. I can just imagine God saying to the Holy Spirit, "Okay, remember that it is Rich we are dealing with. He is slow, so we will have to repeat things a few times to make sure he gets the message."

It became very clear that there was a very significant change that would happen when I was about fifty-five years old. I had no idea what this would be, and God was not talking. But this was still a few decades away, and I did not have a clue as to the nature of what was going to happen, so I did not give this too much thought except for obeying what I was told. I thought that God wanted me to retire early and spend the rest of my life living it up. Goes to show how little I knew about God. And regarding what did happen, was I ever wrong.

Somehow, the event of that time in the future also required more wealth than my career at Hewlett-Packard could provide. This sounded really strange and out of this world. Why was I being told and urged to prepare for something that was going to happen thirty years beforehand? It all seemed so surreal. Because of the oddity of this, I never told anyone until after the event happened. It was only then that all the pieces fell into place, and I finally understood what everything was all about. Knowing that I had to start preparing was all I knew, and by this time, I was in my early thirties. At the time,

I suspected that God was behind my urgings. These urgings did lead me to not only become a real estate broker but also to become a larger investor in rental real estate, as well.

But the years went by, and we were a very happy family. We had three great children, and God led me to change my mind about where they would go to school. I no longer wanted them to go to public school, and instead, all my children went to a Catholic school in Santa Clara. Two of my children also went to Santa Clara University, a Jesuit Catholic university. The first one of my children to get married was my son.

What Did God Reveal of Himself?

1. The spirit world is very real. All of us came from the spiritual realm and were at one point just like the little spirits I saw preparing to be born. We all were just like my first grandchild as I saw her months before she was born.

2. While we are living our lives in this physical realm, God is continually with us and guiding us, many times without us even knowing it. From my life experience, I now know that God understands what is to come. If we open our minds and our hearts to his guidance and act accordingly, we will be prepared for events yet to come. This does not diminish our free will.

3. Although hardship and suffering is part of life, God wants us to be successful in dealing with it and will give us the grace, strength, and wisdom to deal with it.

4. God also knows what is going on in our heads. When I look back at the angel on the streets of Honolulu and the enormously loving being on the airplane, I can come to no other conclusion that God loves each of us dearly. He will do what is necessary to gain our attention. He sure got my attention with the loving spirit in that airplane above the

Pacific Ocean. Oh, how I wish I could always feel the intense love that the spirit being emanated toward me that afternoon. It was beyond description, and its magnificent intensity is beyond words.

5. We really are, in essence, spiritual beings. We are spiritual beings having a human experience. The real reality lies within the spirit world and not the physical world. This may be hard for many people to accept, but it is definitely true from everything I have experienced. Albert Einstein is quoted as saying, "Physical reality is an illusion, albeit a very persistent one."

CHAPTER 4

Then It Happened

The Unexpected

Nine months after my retirement, the most crushing blow of my life happened. I could have never imagined that this could happen, but it did. I think that we are all like this. It always happens to someone else and not you or someone you love. I think this mindset is something that God allows to help us cope. Like they say, shit happens, but we always believe it happens to someone else. But sometimes it does indeed, like a bolt out of the blue, happen to you. And so it did with my wife and me.

She started to have unusual symptoms and went to the doctor to get checked out. The next day, the doctor called and said she needed to go to the emergency room right away because of her blood test results. She was bleeding, and we did not know from where. She was in the hospital for two days until they found the exact cause. When they found the cause of the symptoms, my life changed in a single instant. Like mystical experiences, this was an event that was burned into my memory instant by instant. I remember every detail of the hospital setting.

I was sitting on a chair next to a nurse's station, and her room was directly across the hall. I was worried sick. My stomach was in knots, and I felt nauseous. The doctors came to her room with some portable test equipment. I had no good feelings at all about this situation. The event I feared most was exactly what happened. It was the diagnosis of cancer for my darling wife. I remember the doctor walking across the hall to where I was sitting, and he told me he had found a cancerous tumor in her colon. Everything turned black. Everything faded away. I no longer heard the normal clatter of a hospital ward. I could see no humans. I could not sense the chair I was sitting on. Time stood still as I was in a state of shock, with my stomach starting to churn with a sickening feeling. Everything turned gray and went out of focus. In the background, I heard the doctor telling me some other things, but all I could hear was that my wife had cancer. Nothing else existed for me—nothing.

Then I put my head in my hands, and in a flash, I saw a vision of a road in front of me. That road was a dark one. I saw what looked like dead trees on either side of it, like something you would see in a horror movie. The road had some twists and turns to it. It led to blackness at the end. This picture of a road I saw had a visual stench to its appearance. There was no "place" where the road ended, just a blackness where the road disappeared into nothingness. It was a horrible sight. There was a very stark reality about what I was seeing. Unlike dreams, where things are foggy and cannot be remembered, I saw everything with crystal clarity. That vision remains with me to this day and is just as fresh as it was so many years ago when I had it.

There was no mistaking this mystical vision I saw. It was a divine vision given to me to prepare me for what was to come. It was as real as everything around me in that cancer ward. I was given to know by God through that vision that her illness was terminal within a second or two of learning her diagnosis from the doctor. My darling wife was going to die of cancer, and there was nothing I could do to prevent that outcome.

I went into a state of shock as my world crashed in around me with no escape except to live through what was coming. My body seemed to go into convulsions and shuddered within, and all I could see was blackness, even while all the normal activities of a hospital were going on around me. I was thrust into a world of pain and agony that was a world for only me that evening as people were walking about and talking to one another, completely oblivious of my inward collapse and pain. No one seemed to notice my tears dripping on the hospital floor and on the inside of my glasses.

Yet strangely enough, in this state of shock, I seemed to feel the presence of God as if he were very close to me, watching me and participating in my pain. I did feel God's presence through my agony as if I were caught between two realms, though, the spirit world and the physical world. The solace of the spiritual realm did not last long, however, nor did it make me feel any better. The wretched agony was so powerful that it drown out and killed any feelings other than my heart being shredded apart into so much wreckage.

Sometimes, I think that people believe that if they sense God, all the good feelings will come flooding back. Well, that is not always the case. In this moment of grief and terror, God was there, but I just felt like throwing up all over the hospital's nice, clean waxed floor. Jesus promised that He would always be with us, but He did not promise he would take away the pain. None of my anguish was removed that evening. The shaking, trembling, nausea, heart palpitations, deep feelings of complete terror, and a strange numbness completely overtook my entire body. It was the most horrible feelings I ever had in my entire life. Everything was doom, complete doom, with no hope for anything that would lessen the agony of it all.

Then the physical world pushed aside the spirit world, or at least my sense of it, and I had to begin to respond to what was happening with my wife. It was then that I felt very alone. That feeling of aloneness was overwhelming. I was alone in the universe. Ever feel alone in a crowded place? I could not relate at all to any of the people in the hospital. It was as if no one was there, only me, by myself with the acid of terror welling up within my inner being. It would be up to me and only me to make all the right decisions and hide the terror inside my heart. I knew it would be this was for years to come. Everything regarding her cancer treatment would be up to me and the doctor. I would be responsible for executing all aspects of her treatment while trying to save her life futile as it would be. But I knew I was destined for failure no matter how well I did what I had to do.

This was a mixture of horrific and torturous emotions along with feelings that God was with me. There seemed to be some kind of eternal quality to what was happening. In some respects, it was as if I were in a movie as a character playing a painful part. It was so real while the spiritual realm was also open at the time, too. Somehow, the two realms were present at the same time. But I was stuck in this movie in the real world, wanting to escape to the spiritual realm. I wanted to go back home there. But I knew I could not.

After some unknown length of time, I somehow summoned the strength to get off the chair, walk across the hall, and see Marilyn my wife. She was knocked out by some drugs and would not be up until the next morning. All I could do was go home—alone, empty, and in the darkness of the night. As I walked to the parking lot, nothing existed, nothing except the burning shreds of my heart and soul inside me and this fleshy lump of clay that imprisoned me slowly making my way to the car. I heard nothing during that forsaken walk, no sound, no feeling, no sight really, nothing but my tears falling on the floor as I realized I did not know where the car was. I would have to put a happy face on things for the benefit of my children waiting for me to tell them what happened, and there were many questions aimed at me. I have no memory of getting home that night, nothing about walking out of the hospital, and nothing of going to my car where ever it was when I found it or driving home. All that disappeared into the blackness of that time.

Then began my acting career. I knew now that I had to become a happy-faced actor and hide all the wretched agony that was seething in my heart, boiling my soul, and stabbing my heart with the knives of knowing what was to come. I had no idea that I would have to do this for a little more than five years.

It was a long time after thinking about things that I knew for sure why God had urged me for all those years to invest as I did. The money was not for fun and games. Rather, it would be needed to allow me to be with my darling wife all during her sickness and pay for treatments not covered by insurance. I was able to be with her around the clock because of listening to what God encouraged me to do thirty years prior to prepare for this horrible event. We could give her all the advanced treatments available, and I could be by her side, taking care of her every hour of the day and night since I did not need to work anymore. It was this that God was preparing me for during the past thirty years, and all the while, I had no idea of what was going to happen. But God certainly did. I was able to connect the dots, and in looking back, I could see the fingerprints of God on the journey that my life took.

The Bible says that we need to have faith and that "all will be revealed to us" Corinthians 2:10. And so it was with me. I finally knew what the real plan was and why I got those urges so many years prior. I remain thankful that I had enough faith to follow the nagging instructions God was giving me—I do not know how I would have been able to work in a high-pressure marketing job in a computer company and take care of my wife and family. As it was, I would now be a full-time caregiver.

Over time, our family had gotten used to Mom being sick. It became a regular feature of our lives. My children were now old enough to help with some of the care Marilyn needed. My oldest daughter was about thirty. But they all were either going to school or working full time. So I was the main care giver. I was just glad that we had the means for me to do that. Countless doctor visits, hospital tests, and a myriad of medicines to be administered became our way of life. After her first surgery to remove the tumor, everyone but me was optimistic. Even her oncologist was feeling good about the new prognosis. But knowing the future can be a terrible burden. It can rob you of any happiness when seemingly good news is heard. And as foretold, the cancer made a comeback after about a year. It came back with a miserable shocking vengeance. That was the beginning of the downhill slide. But we tried to maintain a regular family life as best we could. However, my wife was beginning to get weaker and weaker. I so admire how she coped with all the treatments and other stuff.

Even though I was told by the eternal spirit world how things would turn out, I still would stop at nothing to avoid Marilyn's sickness ending in her death. So I did another thing for her that I know helped a lot. I became a Reiki master. I gave her Reiki treatments every day without fail. Now Marilyn did not necessarily believe in this stuff but I knew better as I could feel the energy flowing through me and into her. It was God's healing energy that I could feel. At times it was so strong that I began to sweat so much that drops of sweat would drip off the end of my nose as I bent over her with my hand placed on her main chakras.

Most times I gave her Reiki, I could now see spirits around us. There were usually somewhere between five to ten watching as she laid on the bed while the treatment progressed. It was during this time in my life that my gift of seeing spirits grew to what it is today. God blessed me with this Karim and I treasure that more than any physical possession I have.

Most people with the kind of cancer that Marilyn had last two to three years at most. My darling wife lasted more than five years. I strongly attribute that to all the prayer and Reiki I was able to give to her. Many people prayed for her too I know and that also made a tremendous difference as well. Never underestimate the power of prayer.

The days, weeks, and months dragged on and on. The rhythm of the house and the children settled into the regularity that all families have. We were no different. The big difference was all the medical equipment that seemed to keep on coming and all the medicines I kept on a stand in the upper hallway. Nonetheless, things were progressing, and I was beginning to wear out from all the stress and uncertainty and hoping against hope that what I was told years before would not be the final outcome.

What Did God Reveal of Himself?

1. God is sovereign over all physical reality. He has complete dominion and control of everything we perceive with our senses. He is Lord of both the seen and the unseen. I knew for certain that if it was the will of God to heal Marilyn, He could have done so. But for reasons I will not know until my time here is done, things were supposed to happen this way. How does a person live with the knowledge that his wife is going to die regardless of all the happy talk that goes on with friends and family? One thing is to become a good actor, and I did. I got to be such a good actor, hiding the depression in my heart, that I could be talking with you and you would not know the extent of the agony I was experiencing.

2. We don't always get what we want. We just have to take it on faith that God really does know best, and if He says no, then rest assured that it will somehow turn out for the better doing things and accepting things His way. I still have a hard time with this one, even when I really do know it is true. I have yet to understand why my wife died so young, leaving me in a trash pile of tormented emotions.

3. This life on earth is meant to be difficult and includes suffering. God is aware of all of it. He knows exactly where we are, what we are thinking, and what we are doing every split second of our lives. How else could he have known I was in that bedroom in my house as I performed Reiki?

4. Think about this, dear one: God knows everything and is everywhere all the time. One of the apostles said that no matter where he went, there is no place where God is not.

5. Although God did not directly reveal this, I can't help but think that this life on earth is important. In the greater eternal scheme of things, though, it is the spiritual life or the spiritual realm that is what is really the most important. If we are eternal

spiritual beings having a human experience for learning and spiritual growth, then anything that happens here cannot hurt us as spiritual children of God. Yes, it will certainly seem like it while we are incarnated in the physical world. But once we go back home, we will bring with us new experiences and knowledge that we did not have before we came here. With these new experiences, we will have made spiritual progress growing closer to God our Father. In doing so, we will be able to partake in higher and higher levels of ecstasy, love, and intimacy with God himself. Looking back at our lives will make it seem like it was all worth it. I ask you to think about this.

CHAPTER 5

Five Years of Fighting a Terrible Cancer

Becoming a Reiki Master

During her illness, I became a Reiki practitioner and later a Reiki master. My motivation for doing this was simple—to heal my wife any way I could. I never forgot the vision I had in the hospital when the doctor told me about her tumor. I was still sickened with the knowledge that she would not survive this. But I was not going to just give in. I would exhaust myself completely if it would give her a better chance. I gave her Reiki treatments every day.

During these treatments, I had many mystical experiences where I saw divine spirit beings gathering around us as I served as a conduit for God's life-giving energy. It became very normal to sense and, almost every time, actually see spirit beings around her bed as I performed the Reiki treatment. At times, there were as many as fifteen to twenty spirits watching me give her God's life energy through Reiki. Divine beings and angels are always attracted to events of those who are performing God's work through intense love of another person and performing God's will.

How did it look like to see spirits? It was not like seeing a person in the room with us. My eyeballs were of no use. It was much better than that—much better. Rather, it was like seeing an image that somehow bypassed my eyes and was formed directly in my mind. I could close my eyes and still see the spiritual being, whether it was an angel or some other heavenly being like Martin. The strangest thing was that it did not matter where I pointed my eyes. I could see spirit beings behind me as if they were in front of me.

As I wrote these words, I could see one large angel off to my right about five feet away. It was a big angel who has accompanied me for a long time. I believe he or she was here to protect me from the dangers I face in everyday life. The angel remains with me to this day. My spirit guide, Martin, is also here and is feeling somewhat frustrated for I keep forgetting to include him in more of my decision-making processes. For that, I apologize, Martin.

The appearance of the spiritual beings is always transparent and is so during a Reiki session as well. I could also see the walls, furniture, and pictures on the walls through them. Most of the time, I could not make out the details of their faces, but I could definitely perceive their general body characteristics, what they wore, and their outline. Many wore robes, but some wore other kinds of clothing, more like what we would wear here on earth. Yes, I also did see the angel have wings in in a folded position. Some of them appeared significantly larger than a normal person would be. They were white, and some had gold around them.

All of them were higher than floor level. For some reason, they always appeared higher in the room than someone would if they were standing on the floor. When I saw many spirits, it seemed that the ones in the second row appeared higher than the ones closest to me. Stadium seating? I do not know.

Jesus Comes in Peace and Divine Love

Have you ever wondered if Jesus Christ would ever bother to visit you in person? Most people I talk to have never even had this question come to mind. Their assumption is that Jesus is in heaven, we are here, and He left 2,000 years ago. Yes, He was crucified and resurrected on the third day and will come again. It is those last words that leave people to think that Jesus is in Heaven and will someday come again, but no one knows when that will be. In the meantime, He is not here but up in Heaven. Well, I have good news about whether Jesus would come to visit us individually here on earth. I can tell you that the answer is yes. God continues to be intimately concerned and involved with each of our lives, and yes, God continues to work through our Lord Jesus Christ today and in the future. Jesus has never stopped appearing to people. I know for certain this is true because it happened to me. Yes, you read that correctly. Jesus did indeed come to visit during a Reiki session I was conducting for my wife.

As fantastic as it may seem, Jesus Christ visited us and was standing on the other side of the bed where my wife was while I was giving her Reiki and praying. I know that this sounds too good to be true, but my testimony to you is that our Lord and Savior was standing there across the bed from where I was kneeling. He was so very peaceful, and I sensed that He was very pleased with what He saw. Our Lord decided to appear to me in the classical manner like we see Him in the movies. Perhaps He chose to appear this way so I would have no difficulty recognizing Him. I do not know. His dark brown hair was long, shoulder-length. He wore very simple white robes. But they seemed brighter, whiter, and cleaner than the way His dress appears in the movies. I could not see his feet because the bed was in the way. Jesus stayed for a few minutes. He remained still with His head bowed in prayer. He did not say anything. Jesus was praying for my wife and probably for me, too.

I cannot begin to describe how that felt, seeing our Lord of the Gospels standing there in the bedroom, praying as I delivered God's healing energy to her. I was not startled or surprised. In fact, I was surprised that I was not surprised. It seemed so natural, so right, and so proper to see Jesus standing there with us in that sacred act of delivering God's healing energy. It just seemed so very natural to me.

There was such a quality of closeness and love that permeated the air that afternoon. It was also as if things were unfolding as they should no matter how horribly painful they were. This seems so very odd to have written that last sentence. Yet it is true, painful—horribly painful—but it is as should be. How can it be that with our understanding of God's unconditional love, the love Jesus has for us, and what we know of the kingdom of heaven that pain and agony in this world that God created would be considered "as it should be"? That is a mystery that I will carry with me for the rest of my days.

I remember saying to Jesus, "Thank you, Lord." That was all I could get out of my mouth—well, actually my brain, as this is what I told him in thought. I told Marilyn, "Jesus is here with us, darling." She was unimpressed and not really comprehending the wonderfulness of what was happening. She was too sick to appreciate anything, frankly. He was just so peaceful, and I knew without a doubt that He was pleased with what I was doing. I also felt that things were under control and happening as they were meant to be. I knew He was with us during this awful time. It seems to me that when things are the worst, we are the closest to heaven, and Jesus is never more than a few feet away. It felt horrible to see my wife so sick, but at the same time, there was peace in the room that emanated from Jesus Christ standing there. I felt so much grief of that which was to come while also experiencing the peace and love of Jesus at the same time—two opposite perceptions and emotions coexisting in my heart. Yes, the Gospels are true, and Jesus is indeed the way, the truth, and the light. He proved that beyond any doubt that afternoon in that bedroom with His divine presence here in real life as the two of us were living it. I was so very blessed to actually see Jesus appear that afternoon while attending to the needs of my very ill wife.

The Divine Spirits around Us Every Day

After becoming a Reiki master and treating my wife, I began to physically be able to see divine spirits, as well. To this day, I can see them when I am peaceful and let my mind float toward the spirit world. My wife could, too, toward the end of her illness. One time I was standing next to her bed in our house, and she said that a man dressed in a sweater walked by the foot of her bed and passed right through me as if I was not there. To me, this marked the time when she was beginning her transition into the spirit world. She was beginning to see things that belong in the spirit world. She was never able to do this before. She plainly saw a spirit being walk right through me. I did not feel or see anything as it happened. But she saw it clearly and told me about it.

I want to repeat some things about spiritual sight that I feel is very important. One very interesting fact about being able to see spiritual beings is that there is no need to have your eyes open or to be looking in a particular direction to look and see them. Spiritual vision is not like seeing within the limitations of your eyes. You can see them even if they are behind you. Spiritual vision is omnidirectional. There is no need to turn your head to see something from the spirit world. After my wife passed away, she has always appeared to me right behind my right shoulder, and I can see her as clearly as if she were physically standing in front of me. That continues to this day. Since her death, her chosen appearance has evolved into something so beautiful it is hard to describe. Yet no matter how she appears, there is never any doubt that she is my wife of thirty-eight years. More recently, as my life continues on, her direct appearances are becoming less frequent.

Being Pulled Out of My Body

Two years before my wife passed away, she was still strong enough to go on a Caribbean cruise with the whole family. It was a wonderful trip for the whole family, except me, since I had known what was going to happen. I knew that time was starting to run out, and there was no avoiding what was going to happen. There was a horrible stark contrast between the beauty of the ship and the Caribbean versus the shattered pieces of my heart. I could not stand the emotional pain

I was in while trying to smile knowing what I knew. One of the hardest parts for me on the ship was hiding when I was crying my eyes out and dry heaving. Then I would start coughing so hard that I felt like my lungs would come out. This triggered my asthma, and I would have difficulty breathing. Sometimes someone would notice my breathing, and I would pass it off as the humid air bothering me. I did not have an appetite to speak of, so at least I would not leave a mess on the floor.

While on the cruise, I kept getting strong urges to go to the chapel, which was on the top deck toward the rear of the ship. I really did not want to. I felt going there was just asking for more than I could take. Hadn't I suffered enough these past three years? Now God wanted me to go and pray. Shit! What good would that do? But on the fourth day, I finally went. It was a small, beautiful chapel. It was shaped in a semicircle with little private enclaves surrounding the circumference of the circle. I could sit there and not be seen. I was the only one there.

After praying for some time and crying, something completely unexpected happened. Never in my theological training or mystical experiences would I have imagined what happened next. Without any warning, feelings, or anticipation, I was literally and suddenly taken out of my body. It was as if a gentle yet very strong hand had wrapped itself around me and removed me completely out of my physical body. I had absolutely no control over what was happening to me. This was something completely new. I was not the least bit scared, and I did not suffered any discomfort at all. This tremendous force accelerated me upward at a fantastic rate of speed. I was going ever faster and faster. Everything became a blur. I had no idea where I was going, but I knew that this was of God. Yes, I instantly knew that I was being summoned by powerful divine beings close to God. There was no mistaking the fact that I was now out of my body and traveling at a tremendous speed toward a place unknown. I became spirit with no physical body or bodily sensations.

I was no longer on a cruise ship in the Caribbean. I had absolutely no fear, but rather a deep sense of peace came over me. I remember saying "Thank you, God" as I was speeding ever faster and faster toward my unknown destination. After a few moments, I found myself in the presence of two divine beings who were dressed in white robes. Unlike almost everyone in heaven who is young-looking, they were older-looking and looking at me peacefully.

Without words, I knew they wanted to hear what I had to say about my wife's sickness. I pleaded with them to spare her life and return her to health. I knew without a doubt that they had the power to perform what we call miracles, and this is what I begged them to do for her. I pleaded and pleaded with them. I said things like, "What use is it for her to die? She needs to live. Please spare her, please." I said other things like that, as I was crying and begging for her life. After saying everything I could think of, these two divine beings looked at each other, and with great speed, they went upward where I could not see them anymore. A moment later, I found myself back in my body on the ship in the chapel. I did not sense any kind of speed returning to my body. It was as if one moment I was with these two divine beings and the next I was back in my body.

They did not communicate anything to me, which I found profoundly disappointing. Actually, I got very irritated and upset and disappointed that these two divine beings yank me out of my body and then say nothing to me about my wife or any good words of love or encouragement. Perhaps I remain a rebel in some divine ways, but when my time comes, I want to talk with these two divine elders and find out their story why they did not say anything or give me some morsel of peace in my heart.

I interpreted their lack of any reassurance or kind words to indicate that they really did not want to be with me but were told to do so by God himself. I knew from their reaction to what I told them that nothing was going to change the destiny of my dear wife. I have to be completely truthful here and say that I did not like these two divine beings at all. At least they could have said something to me and perhaps reassure me that although nothing was going to change, they could have said that she was going to be in heaven to be very happy and that she would communicate with me. But no, they did not utter any such thought or word to me. I still feel they were rude, frankly. I plan to take this up with them when my time comes. Perhaps that will be like an ant bossing around an elephant. Maybe they thought I was whining too much. I do not know.

But I am very grateful that God sent these two powerful divine beings to pull me out of my body and listen to me. I was given a fair hearing but to no avail. One day, I will know why they said nothing to me. Needless to say, it was terribly difficult for me to hide my anguish during the remainder of our vacation. I tried not to spend much time with my wife for the few remaining days of the cruise. I would sit on the balcony pretending to read. My wife would be with other members of the family doing things around the ship. Any joy of the beautiful water, scenery, and shipboard activities evaporated into a dull stabbing ache in my heart with more dry heaves while crying that made smiling next to impossible.

What does one do when heavenly spirits say no? Just what do you do? When you are given knowledge of something in the future, it becomes both a blessing and a terrible burden. Knowing the future gives you the opportunity to do all the right things to continue to prepare for what will happen. But the knowing also is in itself a horrible burden that consumes you in your mind, body, and spirit. Knowing the future requires you to become a good actor and learn very quickly how to hide your inner torment so as not to transfer that burden to others that you love. I learned how to cry and sob silently and quickly wipe away the tears, use Visine to take the red out of my eyes, and look normal within about two minutes. If I did not look right, I would always blame it on my allergies. This is how I lived my life for years.

What I was told on the ship was consistent with my vision of the road leading into darkness in the hospital years prior. The events were unfolding as they were told to me that they would. I fought it every inch of the way to no avail.

The Final Hospital Visit

During her final stay in the hospital, several divine mystical events occurred. If anyone ever needed proof of a loving God who always is with us, no matter how dire the situation is, these events should bring comfort to them. This is why I am writing about this as God has asked me to do. Tell the exact truth of the divine mystical events that occurred in my life and the hospital during my wife's last stay there.

She had almost died three times due to complications from the aggressive chemotherapy treatments and radiation she was receiving. If I was not with her all the time, she would have died a few years earlier. One time, she went from a normal temperature to 103.8 in a matter of ninety minutes. Had I not been with her, she would have died. This is another blessing of God by His guidance decades earlier resulting in my early retirement and being able to be with her. She wanted to stay with her family as long as she could, in part to see our first grandchild, Isabella, continue to grow up. I was determined to make that happen for her. Her other grandchildren we not yet born when she passed away.

However, after a few days in the hospital treating her for a life-threatening blood infection, I was sitting by her bed, and she asked me if I could see two guys sitting by the entrance to the bathroom. I could not see them, but I instantly knew who they were. They were angels waiting to take her to heaven. She could clearly see them, but I could not. I looked in their direction and asked them if they would allow me to see them. Nothing happened; I was not being allowed to see what she was seeing. Now at the time, she was completely lucid and had all her senses about her in a normal way. She was not suffering from any kind of delusion or medically induced fantasy. The only medications she was on were a cocktail of powerful antibiotics. The fact that she could see these divine spirit beings (angels) and I could not is completely normal for mystical experiences. Remember my encounter with a divine being of light in the jet over the Pacific Ocean? I could see the divine entity, but no one else could. It is no surprise that my wife could see the two angels and I could not, although I felt really disappointed that I was not given permission to see them.

I asked her to describe them to me. She said the two angels were dressed in white, they had very peaceful looks on their faces, and one of them had curly hair. One had blue eyes. She also said that although they looked like males, they had an effeminate appearance about them. They were very peaceful and patient and were just sitting there waiting. She also told me that they had been there the day before, but she told them to go away. They did at her request. But the next morning when I was there, they came back and resumed waiting. I knew that her time on earth was very short now. There was no other explanation.

My Mother's Vision

I slept in my wife's hospital room that night and was woken the next morning by a commotion where she was sitting on the edge of her bed, trying to rip out the tubes she was connected to. The nurses came quickly, and I calmed her down, and it was decided in the next five minutes that she should be taken home. The hospital could do nothing else for her. A few minutes later, my cell phone rang. It was my mother. She was upset and told me that she had had a vision that Marilyn was ripping out her tubes and that she was very upset about that.

Yes, about fifteen minutes after she was trying to rip off her tubes, my mother calls me with a vision of exactly what was happening. My mother saw all this as it happened and then called me. Now stop and imagine this for a second. Your own mother suddenly has an awful vision of your sick wife in the hospital trying to rip out her tubes because she has had enough suffering. She saw what was happening as it actually happened. These kinds of visions happen all the time throughout the world. We do not hear much about these things because most people pass them off as either too weird or just one of those things. Well, it is not just one of those things as this is a strong lesson that we are all connected in a loving matrix. Things that happen can be sensed and seen by others many miles away. There is no distance in the way we think of it in the spirit world. This is a wondrous divine experience that happened exactly as I describe it.

Were it not for my unconscious following of God's guidance during the preceding thirty years, we would not have been prepared to deal with my wife's needs due to her fatal illness. I shudder to think how things would have been if I had to work while she was fighting her illness. God spared us from that. My time caring for her was a five-year battle against cancer that ultimately took my loving wife away from me. It was a battle of horrific emotions, drugs, love, and ultimately death.

Her Spirit Leaves This World

She came home that day and was ever so happy to be out of the hospital. After a few days, I thought that something might happen that evening or night, so I told my kids that I was sleeping in Mom's room and that they were to stay out of the room until the next morning. Then a few hours later, it happened. She was by my side the moment she passed away. She went to heaven silently without moving a muscle. She did not move a muscle and had been sleeping for a few hours. One minute, she was slowly breathing and then that faded away in the most peaceful way one can imagine. I was at the foot of her bed watching TV with the volume down very low, so I could hear the slightest sound. In the silence of the evening, something caught my eye on my right side. I looked in her direction to see what it was. At that very moment, God allowed me to see her spirit depart her body and slowly float away toward the ceiling and go through it where I could not see her anymore.

It is so very hard to describe the indescribable. But I could see her spirit and see through it at the very same time. Her spirit was transparent, but I could see her as she ascended away from me into her eternal bliss with God in heaven. Risking the poverty of words that are so primitive regarding pure spiritual phenomenon, I was seeing a small ball of energy that shimmered with life as it slowly rose toward the ceiling at an angle, not vertical, but rising toward the wall to my left and the ceiling at the same time. Her spirit was active. I could see it was alive, pulsating, and moving within itself. There was a certain quality of the color of silver to its transparency. It seemed to slowly ripple across its transparent surface. It took about fifteen seconds to rise ever so gently and silently before I could not see her anymore. I knew she was with the two angels who appeared to her days earlier in the hospital. She was in very good hands, going to a heavenly place where we will all return to with our open minds and hearts loving God during our lives.

In one sense, I was relieved that her years of suffering had ended, and I saw without any doubt that God had taken my darling into heaven to be with him. Then a few moments later, like a horrific dam burst, the realization that I just lost my wife of thirty-eight years hit me with an awful crashing and agonizing ripping at my heart. I started to sob uncontrollably. I closed her half-open eyes and put the blanket over her beautiful head. My first words to her a moment after her passing was a sobbing, "Honey, I can't do anything more for you now!" It was like I wanted to continue taking care of her. Yes, I did want to continue. But now all of a sudden, there was nothing left for me to do for her. I had gone from cancer patient caregiver to widower in a blink of an eye. No more physical caring turned into a tsunami of unrelenting tears of grief and agony that is indescribable. My guts were being ripped out of my body as the nausea, aching in my chest, and spinning room were so violent I wanted just to go with her. Feelings of complete helplessness overwhelmed me, and I turned into a heap of brokenhearted emotions.

At the funeral and after I spoke her eulogy, I did not join the crowd in the social hall to have a bite to eat and greet all the people. I went with the hearse back to the funeral home to be with my darling one last time privately. It was a private room with just the two of us in it. I stood by her casket and cried my eyes out for an unknown length of time. There was my wife of thirty-eight years. To me, she still was the beautiful woman I married so long ago. Then I leaned over the edge of the casket and kissed my darling wife good-bye on her lips for the last time in this physical world and closed the lid. Then I slowly walked out the door, telling the funeral director that I wanted to walk home even after he offered me a ride. It was raining, and I thought how appropriate that was. I did not care how wet my suit got or how horrible I looked. I started to walk home in some kind of fog.

I did not know where I was, and subsequently, I got lost going home. It was night, and I was soaking wet, not knowing where I was and not really caring either. God must have been looking out for me. I did make it home safely, but I am not sure how. All I remember was the rain, getting soaking wet, the darkness, not knowing where I was, being lost on the way home, and then being home somehow.

With this ends a thirty-year story that involved God's guidance, His caring and love for all of us, divine events, and many unforgettable mystical experiences. God prepared me for the most horrible experience of my life without me knowing it. And He especially was looking out for and caring for my wife through me, her children, and my love for her, making it possible for me to take the best care of her.

However, mystical experiences do not stop with the end of this story. They continue on in my life. It seems that the veil between heaven and earth became far more permeable after she died. God decided that I would continue experiencing mystical events for the benefit of others through Reiki sessions and other things that I do including meditation.

What Did God Reveal of Himself?

There are a number of divine lessons that we can learn from this thirty-year story.

1. Each divine event that occurred was part of an overall plan that God had for both of us. If something divine or mystical

occurs that does not make sense, I advise that you pray about it for God's guidance and wait for the next event to occur. Events may not even be considered mystical, but they are probably a part of the divine plan for your life. Wait, observe, and try to connect the dots. Perhaps, then, things may become clearer about our Father's intentions. Many times, events are part of a much larger picture that does not become clear until the final piece is put into place. Do not blindly go through life without discerning the connections of events in your life. Look into your past and see how one thing led to another and learn what there is to learn while being alert for divine will and intentions. Do not be too impatient like me, for God has his own timetable and does not pay attention to our wishes time-wise. God's timing is perfect. Ours is not.

2. God hears all our prayers. It is my belief that it is impossible for God not to hear all our prayers and be aware of all our thoughts and emotions. How else could the mystical events described above happen? Remember this. It is impossible for God not to hear every prayer you ever said.

3. We are all part of a unified brotherhood, inexorably connected by love. This is the only way that my mother could have been aware of my wife trying to rip out her tubes. From my mystical experiences and divine contacts, I have come to believe that distance between us is an illusion. We are all inexorably connected into a tight-knit brotherhood where what affects one person affects all of us one way or another. It is a sad deception to think otherwise. We are also inexorably connected to God in ways that we cannot yet understand. But praying to God can reveal these connections as God in not of secrets but rather he wants to revel himself to all of us.

4. God knows us better than we know ourselves. He has knowledge of us before we were born into this world, and what we do here is part of a continuing relationship we have

with our Heavenly Father. I will tell another story about this later in this book.

5. Each of our lives does have a plan. This plan is developed and agreed to by us before we are born. We all have a special reason to be here and a mission to accomplish that has eternal consequences. No matter how dull and mundane things may seem to be, every life is priceless and unique, with a set of goals that no one else can accomplish but you and you alone.

6. Jesus Christ is not only very real but knows what is going on with our individual lives. How else could He have come that afternoon to pray for my wife while I was giving her a Reiki session? He is a divine person of peace and love and totally giving to all who ask for his help. He actually came that hot afternoon to pray next to her bed while I was giving her the best spiritual living energy from God. Jesus knew that and came to us. I cannot begin to put into words the relationship we have with Jesus Christ other than complete and total love that spans eternity.

7. God has appointed certain highly advanced divine beings to have loving dominion over us humans. They too seem to know what is going on and what we are thinking and our true needs. I say *true needs* because it is only our needs that foster real spiritual growth that really matter. I cite my experience with the two divine beings that pulled me out of my body to let me plead with them for the life of my wife. After that experience, I realized that they already knew what I was going to say and what answer was the spiritually correct one, even though it was terribly painful for me. I will only know why my wife died so early after I myself join the heavenly realm, where all will be revealed. All will be revealed to you regarding your lives.

CHAPTER 6

Death is not the End Rather It's a New Beginning

Proof We Live After This Earth

The following events actually occurred in this physical reality that we all live in. I assure you that what I am going to say is not the product of a grieving husband's imagination. Having been well-educated in pastoral ministry, spirituality, and Reiki has given me the tools to discern the differences between imagination and real divine events. If I had any doubts about the stories I am about to tell you, I would never include such things in this book. Each event revealed herein passes all the tests of reason and the characteristics of real mystical experiences.

Right after my wife died, it was these two thoughts that were my consolation. First, she was in heaven. Secondly, she suffered no more. This gave me some comfort. I felt relief that she suffered no more, but that emotion was tangled up with a bone-deep, chilling realization that my wife was gone and I would never see her again, at least not until I also passed on. But I would happily be proven wrong on this point. I would see her many times in the future. I had no idea this would happen.

Amazingly, my wife appeared in two people's dreams the night she passed away. Both these people were miles from each other. She appeared in vivid dreams that both people told me that there was no mistaking what they experienced. She appeared to my daughter-in-law and my future son-in-law in dreams. She spoke to them in an effort to let the family know that she was doing just fine. Incredibly, both of them heard the exact same words, "I feel so much better now." Thinking about it, what was said makes excellent sense considering that she suffered so very much in the months leading up to the evening she passed away. It was wonderful to know about these two dreams and very validating that she said the exact same thing to two family members as they slept. This was music to my ears, having lived so long next to her and feeling all the suffering she was enduring. If you have ever seen someone accidentally smash their thumb, you can almost feel the pain yourself. This is the way it was for.

These dreams happened about ten hours after her death. Both said they heard her in her own distinctive voice with her Filipino accent. These identical dreams brought the family great joy. My darling wife was alive and suffering no more. This mystical experience was a great blessing and showed God's care for all of us during this kind of awful time in our lives. As terribly painful it was for me to experience the death of my wife, I would have chosen this path for her if it meant the end to her awful suffering and the agony that filled every minute she was here on earth. I would rather suffer the agony of her death than let her experience suffering for one minute longer. When you are married for thirty-eight years, the closeness you develop is a divine gift. What one of you experiences, so too does the other.

During the final phase of her illness, she had an intravenous drip bag full of morphine. It automatically dispensed morphine every fifteen minutes. In addition to this, every fifteen minutes, I could press a button and give her more painkiller. I was determined that she would not suffer pain in her last days. I was successful with this. I erased her pain, knowing that my personal pain would increase dramatically in the few days she had left. My personal feelings of complete emptiness, utter desolation, and total grief would not come until a few weeks after her death. Before that time, I was in a state of shock and numbness. It was as if a horror movie was playing and I was one of the two main characters. It seemed so unreal, but the pain and suffering was all too great and in the center of my consciousness. Then after about two weeks, the reality of what happened began to sink in.

When a person passes over to the heavenly realm, they are very anxious to let their loved ones know they still live and are more than okay. With the assistance of other spirits like their spirit guides, angels, and our own spirit guides, they choose the best way to communicate with those they left behind. Appearing in dreams is certainly a common way for them to do this. In my case that night, I did not sleep at all. The silence was so very loud inside me. So she did not have a chance to communicate with me that way. I could not sleep no matter how exhausted and full of emotional agony I was feeling. The sleeping pill I took had no effect. I just sat on the couch like a zombie, alone with the room, silent, with a feeling of complete deadness in the air that filled my heart with a stinging dread of things to come.

But this is not the end of the story. In a very real sense, it is the beginning of another more loving and exciting story. It is the story of her activities from heaven and through the veil to help relieve the agony her loved ones felt of her death. Marilyn was still with us, and she was about to make multiple attempts to reassure us that she was indeed okay. In my case, I was blessed with the most revelations from her and the most detailed ones. I will discuss these mystical experiences in more depth in the order in which they happened. I learned so much from her about the spirit world, heaven, and the character of God in her appearances and what happened during these events. If you are grieving for a loved one who departed to heaven, I can only say to you to open your heart as wide as you can. Pay attention to possible things that may happen around you that seem odd or inexplicable. They may be your loved one's attempts to communicate with you and tell you they are alive and well.

Life is actually a continuum. It does not end with what we call death. Rather, it is a transition to a higher form of existence where all the troubles with physical existence fall away and we become free from pain and all the other negative things that permeate our lives while here on earth. One of the first things that were validated by my wife is that the teachings of Jesus Christ are true. We do indeed carry on in the spirit and exist in a far better place, provided we have lived a life worthy of ascending to a higher realm we call heaven.

Proof That Your Loved One Is Still with You

In the days, weeks, and months after a person passes away, you can expect to experience some weird happenings, depending on your relationship with the one now in heaven. Much of this depends on just how open you are to mystical things. It also depends on the level of spirituality one has, but that is not totally necessary for a loved one from the other side to do something that says "I am here and very much alive."

I hesitated to write some of these stories in this book because they are very personal. But in the end, I believe that far more good will come from these stories to many of God's loved children. During my recent prayers, I got the direct feeling that God wants to have me tell what has happened to my family members and me since my wife passed away. Everything I am about to tell you has not been changed in any way for literary effect. It happened just as I will describe. It's all real and very mystical. I have had many more very personal mystical experiences with my wife beyond what I will describe now. But the stories I will tell are very representative of the whole of my experiences.

My Wife Shocks My Son with Light

Some people will be like my son, who said regarding spiritual matters, "I will believe it when I see it." He is the Doubting Thomas of the family. He told me that when I had a family meeting a few weeks after she passed away. Others will accept these stories as validation of their own experiences.

Well, regarding my son and his Doubting Thomas attitude, one night, he got what he asked for, big time. In the process, he got the surprise of his life. This happened in our family room where he was sitting, talking on the phone to his girlfriend. Now, in our family room, there is a wonderful display case with about twenty cubicles for artwork. Each cubicle has an individual light that shines down on what's inside. There were beautiful glass sculptures there. My wife kept bugging me to fix five lights that were not working. She wanted the lights on all the time. It did look really good. Since I was always exhausted tending to her needs, I never did fix the lights. Also, I could never find the switch that she hid to turn them on or off when she designed the case. Well, about three weeks after she passed away, Richard had something happen to him that he will never forget.

One evening, my son was alone watching TV in that room and talking on the phone. The rest of the family was upstairs. The display case with the five off lights was behind the TV. Suddenly, all five lights turned on all by themselves as my son was sitting there watching TV. Yes, all five lights suddenly turned on all by themselves! This shocked my son to the bone, and he yelled out, "The lights! The lights!" He got really scared and ran upstairs to get my daughter to show her that the lights were now on. Later, he said he had goose bumps all over his body. It really did shake him up. There is no doubt that my wife turned them on that evening. It was her way to get through to him. It vividly showed him that his mother was alive and well in heaven and that there really is a spiritual realm that we cannot see with our eyes. Those five lights remained on for a very, very long time. We wouldn't dare touch them. After a loved one passes away, it is these kinds of things that are expected to happen in one form or another.

I need to add that for her to turn on those lights, I have to conclude two additional thoughts about the spiritual world. First, what we do and what we think are definitely known in the spiritual realm. Otherwise, how would she know what Richie said about only believing his mom was okay if he saw it somehow? Second, beings in the heavenly realm have some kind of ability to manipulate what exists in the physical world. Otherwise, how else could those lights be turned on like that? It is important for you to consider this when you ponder miracles described in the Bible, or for that matter, the man I met on the street in Honolulu. The inescapable conclusion I come to is that the heavenly spirit world and our physical world are intermingled in ways that we do not understand. It is certainly okay not to understand how as long as you know it is real and believe it is true as this testimony indicates. You would be wise to live your life accordingly.

Marilyn and I had a very deep and soul-entangled relationship. We both felt strongly that we were partners of some kind for eternity. This is true for others of my very close friends, as well. They, too, are soul-entangled with me for eternity. One very special woman named Evangeline and I are also soul-entangled with a very loving relationship that will last past our existence on this earth. I am the luckiest guy on the planet, dear ones. I believe that loving relationships on this earth continue into the spiritual realm.

True love can never be destroyed. Please ponder on this point for it is an extremely important one. Love cannot be destroyed. It by its very nature is eternal. There are laws in physics that say that nothing is lost when something goes through a transition to another form. This also applies to loving relationships. They continue in our lives as we transition back to the spiritual realm from which we all came in the first place. This is the case for all true loving relationships. It is true with Evangeline and me. It is true for all my loving relationships and all of your loving relationships, too. Think about just how absolutely magnificent that is to experience for all eternity.

Miracles do occur. Something spectacular has happened in my life that I did not expect even though I yearned so badly for it. I have met another soul with whom I have become deeply entangled through joyous love. Her name is Evangeline. She will soon become my wife.

I cannot believe how lucky I am to become married to this wonderful woman. As you may remember from the back cover of this book, I am a pastoral minister with a graduate degree. How wonderful is God that allowed me to meet Evangeline, a professor of theology. She taught theology at The University of Santo Tomas in Manila, Philippines. We, too, are soul-entangled for eternity through our deep love for each other. There will never come a time when our love for each other will dwindle. Rather, across the coming eons, our love will grow as God wills it for us.

This is true for all people who truly love someone else. Love creates eternal relationships. It creates eternal families, too. It creates eternal relationships that form the very fabric of creation. When two people are in love with each other and one dies, the remaining one has a very hard road to travel. The one left behind needs spiritual help along the way or bad things can happen. In my case, God has increased the number of my spirit guides, and I have the number of angels increased to protect me also. God will give us what we need but not always what we want. I cannot help but think that my late wife was involved in arranging the situation where Evangeline and I met, fell in love, and will be married for the rest of our lives. I know that Marilyn definitely approves of Evangeline. She told me so. Yes, part of a soul-entangled loving relationship is that loving communication can flow through the veil that separates heaven and Earth. This allows people who love each other to communicate sometimes when the occasion calls for it. More on this kind of communication later.

My Late Wife Appears Out of Nowhere

One day about three or four months after her funeral, I got the bright idea that I should walk to the cemetery where she is buried. I was feeling as emotionally rotten as a person could possibly be. I had dry heaves, my body muscles twitched, and I ached all over. I had no appetite or energy. I felt like a battered piece of meat lying on the ground with no life at all within me. Everything that I was seemed to be drained out of me as my head ached, and throwing up was only a second away. I am not sure what was worse, the ache in my heart or my head. So I thought being physically close to her grave might make me feel better. I walked to the cemetery. Driving was out of the question in the condition I was in.

Oh my! This was a really bad mistake. It is two and a half miles to the cemetery. I was crying all the way over there. Several times, I had to stop as I could not see where I was going. I was looking through too many tears to see. As I got to her gravesite, I broke down and could hardly stand. My head started to swirl around, nausea engulfed me, my legs started to buckle, and I was about to fall over. I lasted no more than sixty seconds before I just had to leave for home. I was sobbing as I left and kept on crying on the way back until something very powerful and mystical happened. To this day, years later, I can vividly remember every little detail of the event I will describe now.

I was walking down the sidewalk with my head down, looking at my feet passing across the concrete. Tears were falling onto the inside of my glasses. Suddenly, a vision started to form to my right side and up. My eyes were open, looking at the sidewalk through the tears on my glasses, but I saw this cloudlike structure forming above my head where I was not looking. I was not looking at where I was seeing. Yes, this sounds strange, but it is just the way it happened. This was my very first experience with what I call spiritual sight or spiritual vision. You can actually see where you are not looking with your eyes. It is not like peripheral vision, but you look directly at the spiritual being or whatever may be presenting itself from the heavenly realm. In the years since, I have experienced this spiritual vision many times. I have found that you can even see behind you without turning your head in the slightest. It is a wonderful experience to behold.

With this in mind, I saw the most beautiful female left hand descend from the puffy white cloud like it was offering me a helping hand. Her skin was so very smooth-looking, beautiful, and lustrous. She looked like she just had a manicure perfectly done to match her beautiful fingers. I could not help noticing that the hand looked exactly like

Marilyn's hand did when we were first married. Also, she was wearing the most beautiful diamond ring on her left ring finger. It was quite a large diamond that glistened in a light from an unknown source. It was cloudy that day as I was walking home, so this diamond was sparkling from another source of light that I could not see. I took hold of her hand, and it indeed felt exactly like Marilyn's hand. It was not my physical hand I used, but I instinctively used my spiritual body's hand. Yes, we all have spiritual bodies that can be thought of as being superimposed on our physical bodies. This is something that science has yet to discover, and the evolutionists will go nuts over when it is discovered.

I simply thought the action of moving my arm and hand upward to meet her hand, and it happened just as if I were moving my physical body. I did not know that I could do this, but it was as natural and automatic as it would be with my physical hand. I even saw my spiritual arm moving upward to greet her hand as it extended downward.

I slid my hand up her arm past her elbow, and yes, indeed, it was certainly my wife. After thirty-eight years of marriage, one gets to know how your spouse's arm feels like. In telepathic thought, I asked her where the large diamond ring came from. Then she said something totally remarkable and unexpected. She said these exact words in a telepathic communication with me: "It's for all the wonderful things you did for me." This is an exact quote of what she said. I did not hear her voice with my ears but with my mind. The best English word to describe this communication is telepathy. The voice was for sure my dear wife, and she was talking to me for the first time since her death. Her voice sounded exactly as it had when she was alive. Then I told her I loved her eternally. With that, the vision melted away. I have no idea how long this mystical experience lasted as I again lost all sense of time. I was dimly aware that I was still walking as all this happened.

I was so stunned by this spontaneous vision that I did not have the sense to ask her any more questions while I had the chance. But in the coming months and years, I would have many opportunities to have almost all my questions answered. I kept on walking and realized that I was not crying anymore. I did not cry for the rest of the day. This was the first time I did not cry for almost an entire day. I know my wife will be the first person I see when I pass away, along with a few others, as she promised this before she went to heaven. Do not ever be afraid of death. There are many deeply loved ones waiting for you in the divine heavenly realm.

I now know that it is true that love can transcend the veil that separates this physical world and the heavenly spiritual realm. Love passes through the veil in all its magnificence and splendor in order to help those of us in this physical world. If my late wife, with the help of other spiritual beings, can know where I am, what I am doing, and what I am thinking, we all should ponder what greater things our Lord Jesus Christ and God our Father can do for us. I take this mystical experience as proof that both realms, the spiritual and the physical, are inexorably intermingled in such a way that our needs and prayers can be answered for our eternal good. Now this does not mean that whatever we want we will get. The beings ascended into the heavenly realm and God our Father are not short-order cooks for prayer satisfaction. There exists in an infinitely higher wisdom and intelligence that governs how our prayers are answered. But my direct experience with the heavenly realm proves that prayers do indeed get answered according to what is best for us. On that day in Santa Clara, California, walking back from the cemetery, my deepest needs were met unexpectedly in a way that I did not even pray for. What an awesome creation God has built for us, His eternal children.

My Late Wife Did Not Like Golf, But ...

Another important story I will tell you (there are many more) is what happened to me on the golf course. The night before, I prayed to God to allow her to play golf with me the next morning. She did not like golf and was never to be seen with me on a golf course. As a recent widower, it was a very hard struggle to push myself out the door to the golf course. But someone was planning something unexpected for me there as I played with my friends.

As I was walking down the second fairway, I started to feel Marilyn's presence very strongly. Suddenly, it was as if she swooped in toward me from behind and started to hug me with her arms wrapped around my neck. At times, I could even feel her head resting on my right shoulder and her cheek pressed against my cheek. I could even feel her black hair resting upon the side of my head. I cannot begin to describe the peace and joy this brought me that day. We spoke sometimes, but it was usually statements of "I love you" going both ways. I could feel her love for me and just how happy she was. I took my spiritual hand and ran it through her hair, and when I did so, I could see that it was a beautiful black shining in the sun. She had gone back to wearing her hair very long just the way she had when we met so many years ago. Yes, dear reader, this is exactly how it happened that day. I was so peaceful that day that I shot my best score of the year. For you golfers out there, it was a seventy-six from the championship tees. She stayed with me for the rest of the day until I went to sleep that evening. I am truly blessed by God for Him to allow Marilyn to do this for me.

"Death is nothing else but going home to God. The bond of love will be unbroken for all eternity." (Mother Teresa [1910–1997]). The world is full of these kinds of stories. I suggest that you seek them out. They will be a comfort to you in times of loved one's sickness and passing away. And be open to these mystical events happening to you too. Do not think it cannot happen to you as my son believed. The result was the biggest surprise of his life. After that happened, I asked him if he believed in spirits. He replied that he did.

Her Jogging Shoes Jogged without Her

About a month after my wife passed away, I experienced another mystical event that involved the movement of physical objects in my bedroom. About a year or so before she died, Marilyn bought a new pair of Puma running shoes. At that point, she was in no condition to do any running, but she found them comfortable. Due to her deteriorating health, though, she never used them, and they were placed in a bookcase in my retreat area. One morning when I woke up, I found this pair of shoes in the middle of the room directly where I would walk if I had to visit the bathroom during the night. When I went to bed, I am absolutely sure they were in the bookcase and not in the middle of the floor. But there they were in the middle of the floor when I woke up that morning, completely unused, with the inserts still inside the shoes. There is no possible explanation other than a divine force had come during the night and placed them where I found them the next morning. What a wonderful sign from my wife that she was well and continuing to communicate with me any way she could.

She Used My Granddaughter to Send a Message

About five months after she went to the other side, I was again very distraught and dealing with increasing depression, stress disorders, and anxiety. This is something I have had in varying degrees most of my life. After my wife died, my symptoms increased dramatically, and life became a living hell. It was so bad for me that I asked God to just take me now. I did not want to be on earth anymore. The emotional pain was greater than I could stand, with its constant drumbeat of agony and grief. I could stand no longer the daily agony of crying, dry heaves, and a horrible sense that any minute something awful will happen to another loved one. I did not want to leave my room but just take the pills the doctor gave to that alleviated some of the emotional trauma that haunted me constantly. This was so in spite of the mystical experiences I already had. I can be hypersensitive at times, and my wife's death was debilitating for me. I found it harder and harder to function. I wrote books that got published and did fairly well on the market. There was, however, no escape from the feelings deep in the pit of my stomach that not only would I never be myself again but also that all the terrible agonies had become a permanent part of my life.

One day, I really needed more reassurance that she was still with me. I was dealing with intense flashbacks of the evening she passed away. I could still feel her chest being cold when I placed my hand on her breastbone and closing her half-open eyes with my left hand. These flashbacks would come without warning whenever they wanted to. They always triggered horrible feelings of emotional devastation and complete agony filled with blackness that permutated the essence of my complete being. I could not control these flashbacks, and they came whenever they damn well felt like it. I needed to do something, anything, to deal with the emotional terror I had in my heart.

So I got a letter-sized piece of paper and pencil and stuck it to the wall next to my bed. On the paper I wrote to Marilyn, "I love you. Please leave me a message." I was hoping that she would somehow mystically write something on that piece of paper on my wall. I waited for weeks, and nothing happened. Then one day, something did happen.

Sometimes, people and spirits on the other side in the spirit world use people on this side of the veil to do their bidding for them. One afternoon, I walked upstairs into my retreat area and began to sit down. It was then that I noticed that Isabella, my granddaughter, was on the far side of my bed. She never goes there—never. Isabella looked at me like she was going to get into trouble, but I said, "Hi, sweetheart. How is my favorite eldest granddaughter?" She was happy and walked over the thirty feet or so from my bed and hugged me. I hugged her back and asked if she wanted some chocolate. Well, do fish swim? Of course. She got a nice treat.

It was after Isabella walked downstairs that I wanted to see what she was doing on the far side of my bed. There in plain English were the words "I love you, Papa." Now this may seem like not much, but considering my request to Marilyn, the fact that Isabella never comes into my bedroom area past my retreat area, never ever goes to the far side of my bed, and writes me a note in response to what I wrote all adds up to Marilyn guiding Isabella to do exactly what she did on that paper. To this day, that paper hangs on the wall, framed, right where I left it when Isabella wrote on it under the direction of Marilyn. Some may say that I am reading too much into a coincidence. But knowing how the spirit world works within this physical world and knowing how Marilyn had a way of always getting what she wanted when she was with us on this side of the veil, it is absolutely no surprise that she was behind what Isabella did that day. I was so happy and relieved to again have more physical proof that Marilyn was always with me and fulfilling the promise she made to me before she died.

The Years Since

In the years since my wife passed away, our communications have taken on a regular and normal tone to them. We can indeed talk for very brief periods of time with very few words. It seems that most times, she tends to know what is on my mind and will answer even before I get all the words out of my mouth to ask. This is amazing that she knows how I am and what I may be doing. But I do not believe she can see me like other humans do. Beings on the other side do not have a peephole to spy on us. Rather, we appear to them much differently than we appear to each other. Do not worry about being spied on while doing private things. The spiritual world honors everyone's right to privacy, both here in the physical and there in the spiritual.

In the last few years, her appearance has slowly changed. After she first passed through the veil into heaven, she had a solid appearance when I saw her. She wore a white robe then that over time changed into more colorful shades of magnificent pastel colors. Later, she became more translucent in appearance. She would start wearing absolutely gorgeous skirts with different styles of blouses, some with plunging necklines. Wearing necklaces of diamonds became common. Her hair would change length on occasion, as well. More lately, she is wearing it down to her shoulders in comparison to right after she passed away when she wore it very long like when we first met in graduate school.

When she appears to me, she would always be behind my right shoulder. I could see her without turning my head. All I had to do was shift my attention to where she was, and I could see her. Over time, she gradually became more gossamer-looking. It was as if I could plainly see her, but she became more transparent. She always appeared in blue and white that became more flowing with gentle curves. She was becoming increasingly beautiful. She was beautiful to start with, but now her spiritual beauty was increasing to such a level that it is very hard to describe.

At times, she would appear with her hair shortened somewhat, but then the next time, it would be long again. Her skin was now the most beautiful Asian pale white. Her eyes have become slightly more slanted, more like Chinese or Japanese. She is much thinner and is so very graceful when she moves around.

Her clothing has also changed over the years. She now wears robes of indescribable beauty again. The colors range from pastel blues, purples, white, and some pink. It looks like selected pastel colors of a rainbow that shimmer and glisten in the holy light with which she is illuminated.

Marilyn has now become a sometimes visitor. I know she has had other duties to perform in heaven recently, especially since Typhoon Haiyan that hit the Philippines earlier in 2013. She left for a while, and I could not sense or talk to her. But if I really needed her, she would appear in a very few seconds. Such is the divine capability of the heavenly spirit world. It is driven by true love for others. If you are in heaven, needed by a loved one on earth, you will know about it and will respond accordingly. Remember that this physical realm and the spiritual realm are really one continuum separated only by a veil and our ability to perceive, nothing more.

However, I am not sure if it is me or God not allowing as much communication as before, but it seems that my perceptions of Marilyn's presence are getting more far apart. I take this to be normal. This does not bother me, though. It is because I have found a wonderful woman who loves me as I love her. It is a strange experience to lose someone you love so much and for so long in death and then years later have a loving relationship with someone else. I believe that God has provided for me, and I know Marilyn had something to do with this. I know she approves of Evangeline because she makes me so very happy. It is a very strange feeling for me to love my "bringer of light" and miss my wife while at the same time being able to love Evangeline so very much. I guess it is like loving all three of my children at the same time. True love does not die. It continues on as part of our spirit into the higher realms of existence. It is love that holds all creation together, both the seen and the unseen. And as cosmologists and theoretical physicists are finding out through quantum physics, it is the unseen (spiritual realm) that is larger by far than the seen (physical realm).

I continue to rest in the arms of my Father and know that I will see all the people I love who have already gone to heaven like my Grandpa and Grandma Troha and my aunts and uncles. But don't let that sentence fool you. Living this life continues to be a challenge. But with the love of my special sweetheart, I know the rest of my life will be good.

What Did God Reveal of Himself?

1. Somehow, the spirit world knows exactly where we are, what we are doing, and what our emotional conditions are. I cannot tell you how this happens, but I can say for sure that it does. It has been demonstrated so many times in my life. Marilyn passed away only a few hours before she appeared to two family members, telling them she was not only still alive but also doing far better than she had in the physical world. What wonderful consolation for all of us.

2. When Marilyn said "I feel much better now" after she passed away, she was telling us that our physical pains, emotional pains, and all other kinds of suffering drop away as we transition into a pure spiritual existence. What wonderful news this is. But again, this is not really new. The Bible itself says the same thing about heaven. Marilyn just validated it in real life to all her loving family.

3. It seems that it is love that is able to travel through the veil between heaven and earth. If you truly love someone on the other side, talk to that person. You may be surprised when you

get an answer with an open mind and open heart. It is love that holds all creation together in a divine and sacred matrix of kindred spirits where what affects one affects all.

4. Our loved ones will go to great lengths to let us know they are well after their passing to the other side. The running shoes, the turning on of the lights for my son, my granddaughter fulfilling my request to Marilyn, the diamond ring on the ring finger of Marilyn, the clear visits from Cindy, (her story in next chapter) and even Marilyn going to the golf course to surprise me—all these mystical events add up to a deep connection between our earthly physical world and the heavenly realm. These two realms are not independent from each other; rather, they are intertwined in ways that we do not completely understand.

5. Beings in the spirit world can, at appropriate times, manipulate physical objects, like the Puma running shoes and the lights in the family room. Pay heed to these stories and then ponder all the miracles documented in the Bible. These two realms of existence are very close to each other and intertwined in a way to make what we call miracles possible.

6. All these things are real, and they are beyond the ability of physical science to explain them. As a person with a scientific background and having worked at NASA in the planetary exploration branch, I say to never let something scientific push you away from the reality of the spirit world because they say it is not possible. Always remember that science is limited to only those things that are physical and measurable. The spirit world exists beyond what science can measure. Therefore, in science, it does not exist. However, there is one footnote to these comments. In the area of quantum physics, they are getting to a point where reasonable interpretations of experimental data are starting to hint at the existence of God. Perhaps this will be the subject of my next book. It will be a fascinating read if I decide to write it.

CHAPTER 7

A Golf Course Surprise

A Wonderful Surprise on the Golf Course

*I*t had been about a month since Marilyn passed away, and my days were filled with grief and crying for her and her last five years of suffering. We both suffered immensely during her illness. For her, it was being mostly bedridden and in various amounts of pain. I was able to control this mostly using both intravenous and oral morphine. During her illness, for me, it was hiding from the family how horrid I felt both physically and emotionally. I got good at not showing the wreckage on my face after I would have a crying spell and throw up and collapsing on the bed or couch. A caregiver learns to do whatever is needed to keep things going as much as possible for the benefit of others. Not much changed for me after her passing, except things got more intensified.

Uncontrollable crying spells, nausea, and severe headaches along with asthmatic coughing and dry heaves seemed to be the order of many days. I would look forward to being so exhausted from all this; sleeping became a welcome respite from what I endured. Yet, I tried to carry on as normal as I could.

One of my friends invited me to play golf with the regular group I was part of, and I forced myself to say yes. It was extremely hard to drag myself to the golf course that day. After the intense suffering of my wife's death and the horrible loneliness, depression, grief, and terrible bouts of crying, the last thing I wanted to do was get off the couch and go outside. I wanted to hide from this hideous world of pain and agony. But it was a bright and shiny day in Santa Clara. I summoned the courage to drive to the golf course, in spite of my ill health, and saw my good friends waiting for me.

We played the first hole, and I felt like I was returning to an old friend. I had played there so many times over the years. Eight-thirty every Saturday morning was our appointed time. Even though the golf course and my buddies were all so very familiar to me, it was not the same. It was as if I were looking at things through a completely different set of eyes. I was strangely detached from it all, and instead, it was like I was watching a movie that I was in. It felt like I had one foot in the spirit world and one foot here in physical reality. It was so strange to see the same things but perceive them very differently after you have been gone for a while, tending to the needs of your sick wife. I also felt like I did not belong there anymore. There were quite a few months during that winter taking care of Marilyn where I played no golf and was out of touch with my golf buddies. I felt like I was floating while my body was playing golf. I truly was not really there. My body was playing golf, and if someone saw me, they would have seen nothing out of order. But there was so much wrong with what was happening. I was somewhere else while at the same time playing golf. My true self just was not there where my body was located.

I forced myself to smile as best I could and tried to remember which end of the golf club I should hold. I played the first hole in a completely shabby fashion. But then on the second hole, my entire day and demeanor would unexpectedly and dramatically change.

Something wonderful and unexpected was coming my way as I walked down the second fairway. I got about halfway down the fairway, and suddenly I was hit from behind like being rear-ended in a car. A strong force pushed me forward, and I felt that I was being hugged profusely from behind. An aura of happiness seemed to surround me. Although I could see nothing, I immediately knew who it was. It was my darling wife making her first contact with me since she passed away weeks earlier. She wrapped her arms around me and hugged me from behind as I was still walking down this fairway. Nobody watching would ever suspect what was going on with me at the time. But something divine and mystical was happening in the midst of my golf buddies, but they could never perceive what was happening.

To them, everything looked and felt normal, but what was going on was anything but normal. Marilyn and I were reunited where she was able to transcend and cross the veil and back into the physical world where I was so she could hug me, tell me she loved me, and give me the consolation and support I so desperately needed. Believe me, this brought my heart to glowing warmth. She was so happy and was wearing a white robe. Her black hair was the same, and her big, toothy grin was absolutely beautiful. Yes, I could see her hugging me from behind even though I did not need to turn my head.

My darling wife continued to hug me for the rest of my round of golf. Even though she was hugging me, it did not interfere with my golf swing at all. She was in her spirit body, which does not interfere with my physical body at all. She and I talked the whole time. I found out she was living in what we would call a mansion and was very happy there, but she did miss me a lot; I told her I was miserable without her presence and needed her continual support if I was to make it to the end of the my assignment in the physical world.

She told me that she would always be with me no matter what. She told me that I had lots to accomplish in the future and that she would help guide me as no one else could. I thought that was great. Mind you, this conversation was going on while I was hitting shots and sometimes talking to my golf buddies. My darling wife was with me right behind my right shoulder, talking, and I was talking by means of telepathy. I would talk with her only in my mind, she would hear every word, and I could hear every word she was telling me. No one else could hear a word. No one could ever perceive what was going on right under their noses. But there I was, silently talking with my wife who had passed away, being hugged by her and playing golf at the same time.

My grieving and sadness gave way to a certain amount of real happiness in being back with her. I began to feel so calm being with her that I shot a very good score for the eighteen holes even though I had not played for a very long time. Marilyn calmed me down a lot, which allowed me to play my best golf that memorable day.

I feared that she would depart from me forever, but she gave me her word that she would be with me all the days of my life. And so it has been. She has been true to her word to me from that day until now, as I write this. She is with me all the time. We do sometimes have conversations about things that are happening in the family, and she voices her opinion, which at times varies from what she might say if she were still alive. But there are also times I perceive her at a distance away, and all she is doing is observing and not saying anything or responding to me. This is not a case of continual jabbering. Rather, when I really need to talk, she is there. At times, I perceive that she is trying to communicate, but I am not able to receive the message. That can be frustrating. Other times, her message to me is quite clear. The next story about Megan is an example of a very clear message.

Later during this same round of golf, I was playing the twelfth hole. I started to cry while walking by myself separated from my other golf buddies. The realization that I would have to live the rest of my life without her hit me like a ton of agonizing bricks that obliterated my emotions and my heart. I had a hard time trying to hit the ball while crying inwardly and became an emotional mess within a few minutes. Tears flowed down my cheeks and fell to the grass as I walked.

With that, I suddenly and unexpectedly was wrapped within an angel's wings. The angel also approached me from behind and wrapped its wings completely around me. I could actually see the angel's wings surrounding me, giving me strength to endure the pain I was in. This divine angel from God was there to reassure me that God was always with me and gave me strength and calmed me down again while Marilyn was still there giving me her love. This mystical experience of Marilyn making her first contact with me since her death and the beautiful angel wings surrounding me gave me God's reassurance that He was with me through allowing Marilyn to hug me and the angel to surround me with protection and love. Needless to say, it was quite an experience that I will cherish for the rest of my life here on earth.

That day on the golf course set the stage for a continuing loving relationship that will follow me for the rest of my life. The interesting thing that I have learned from this ongoing relationship is that all any departed loved one wants for those left behind is happiness. There is absolutely no ego involved at all. My late wife wants me to have a special love in my life. She wants me to have a woman who truly loves me and who wants to make me happy. She has guided me to a very special woman I intend to spend the rest of my life with, and Marilyn is happy about her. There was another woman earlier who was not good for me, and Marilyn told me so in very clear terms. Yes, it is priceless to have loved ones in heavenly places. Always remember, though, you do, too. His name is Jesus Christ.

What Did God Reveal of Himself?

1. We never know when a spirit being will suddenly appear in our life and basically change everything. In my case, it was re-establishment a thirty-eight-year loving relationship that was interrupted by the death of my wife.

2. Love never dies. It is the immutable force that holds the universe together. It crosses the veil that normally separates this physical world from heaven and the spirit world. In fact, it is only love that is able to penetrate the veil and allow spirits to come here or for our own spirit bodies to travel into the spirit world.

3. Yes, we can communicate with loved ones who have passed on into the heavenly realms, and we can receive guidance from them and of course from God Himself along with the Holy Spirit and Jesus Christ himself. Later on, I have a story about just that.

4. God does not see His creation as we do. He sees it as a continuum where there is a blurred distinction between the physical and spiritual reality. They overlap each other, and this allows one to influence the other and allows beings, for example, in the spirit realm to communicate with beings in the physical world. It is genuine love and openness that allows this to happen. Love is the only thing that flows freely between the physical and spiritual realms.

5. God does not spare his chosen ones from experiencing the hardships of physical life. Frankly, I think actually that things are harder for the chosen ones who are to bring God's words to His other children. Part of this is due to chosen ones being able to see into the glories and unbounded love of God while still on earth. This makes staying here in the physical realm much harder knowing how wonderful the spirit world really is.

CHAPTER 8

Dating Again?

Dating Again? Oh, God, Help Me

There comes a point in widows' or widowers' life where they have to decide if they want to live the rest of their life alone or seek out a loving companion to share the rest of their life with. This is a heart-wrenching decision. At first, I felt like I was betraying my wife. But many of my friends encouraged me to get out there. In my case, I was only sixty years old when my wife passed away. After much prayer, I decided I would see if anybody existed in this world with whom I could share an intimate companionship. Frankly, I doubted there was anybody. But I joined a few dating sites to see what kind of fish there were in the water.

It was almost three years before I decided to date. I went on a large number of coffee dates and got turned off by the caliber and values of the women I met. Frankly, it was awful. Have you ever felt like you were rummaging through a junkyard? I think I set some kind of record for coffee dates. I did not hold out much hope of finding someone who shared my Christian values and was honest and loving. When I met this one lady for a coffee date, I could not stand her in the first few seconds of meeting her. Can you imagine this? It was only a few seconds, and I wanted to immediately disappear. I am sensitive to the energy a person emits, and hers smelled like a sewer burst. God, just get me out of here. That date lasted five minutes, and I just had to get out of there and make up some lame excuse to leave. It became apparent to me that online dating is full of misrepresentations, lies, and exaggerations.

Cindy

Then I saw a profile of one lady who looked promising. I took her out for coffee, and we had a very nice time together. Over the next few months, we became very close friends and enjoyed each other's company a lot. Her name was Cindy. I liked her a lot. And she liked me. I thought this might lead somewhere, and my hopes began to rise a little. But then it happened again. I would have never guessed this. About three o'clock in the afternoon on a Saturday, I called her house to ask her what time I should pick her up to go to the movies. Someone else, whose voice I had never heard before, answered the phone. Immediately, I knew something was very wrong. After finding out who I was, I was told that two hours earlier, Cindy had fallen in the bathroom, hit her head on a sharp object, and died suddenly.

I was again shaken to the core of my soul. I could not believe that I lost Cindy after losing Marilyn. Why would God be so cruel to me? Just how much was I supposed to take anyway? My relationship with Cindy was nothing like that with my wife for sure. But for this to happen again was pouring salt into a very deep wound. I felt like God would rather have another woman die on me than let me date again. Perhaps I was destined to be alone for the rest of my very miserable life.

But little did I know what was in store for me. Starting the very next evening, regular mystical events would occur every night. I would be sitting on the couch watching TV, and spirit beings would suddenly appear behind my right shoulder. One of them was Marilyn, wearing a beautiful white blouse and a translucent blue skirt. But she was standing a little bit farther away from me than she usually did. Closer to me was Cindy. There is no doubt who the spirit being was because I could hear her repeat to me over and over: "Rich, I am so sorry, I am so sorry." You see, Cindy was always afraid that her not so good health would interfere with any relationship she would develop with a man. And for her, the worst happened, which she never ever intended.

Although Cindy was in heaven, Marilyn was helping her contact me. Cindy felt awful about her sudden death. She came to me every evening for at least two weeks, and each time, she would tell me how sorry she was for what happened. I could see the tears running down her cheeks as she stood behind me. I always responded to her by telling her, "It's okay; I understand." Then after a few weeks of her coming with Marilyn standing next to her, her appearances stopped. And I would only sense Marilyn off my right shoulder and slightly behind me. It became time for Cindy to go to her part of paradise and continue her loving existence within the loving arms of God's heavenly realm. I know that she had gone on to her place in heaven. And although I do not have any more contact with her on a regular basis, there are times when I can feel her spirit lightly touching me, smiling, and wishing me the best. But that does not happen very often anymore. Once in a great while, I will get my attention diverted by Cindy just checking on me to see how things are going. I know it is Cindy by the unique energy she has.

Perhaps my grace to have limited contact with the spirit world is God's consolation for me for all the pain, all the trauma, and all the suffering I have gone through in my life, especially over the last decade or more. There are times when I feel like I live my life with one foot in the spirit world and one foot in this physical reality. Frankly, that's a nice position to be in, and I am ever so thankful to God for allowing this in my life. But there is also a harder side to this. I get to see a tiny bit of the heavenly spirit world, and knowing what there is makes it much harder to put up with this physical existence. It can get very depressing at times, being stuck here. This is especially true when I think about the direction in which our world is heading, away from God and toward great suffering, violence, and economic ruin due to greedy governments and citizens wanting the fruits of other people's labors.

Now, one would think that experiencing spirits from the heavenly realm would be more than anyone could ask for. I would agree. Joyfully, my mystical experiences do not stop there. No, much more was to come for me that I would have never expected. Things would begin to become more wonderful and fantastic for me.

Megan

Sometime later, I would meet a woman named Megan on a website. She presented herself as a happy person having gotten over a divorce seventeen years prior. Her husband cheated on her, and she found out after twenty-five years of marriage. She got the marriage annulled through the Catholic Church. I came along, and we had a great time together. One thing that bothered me was that two out of her three children had a bad relationship with her. One child moved to a new house and did not give his new address to his mother. This was a warning sign that I just overlooked as one of those family things that happens. She and I had many nice conversations. But something was still not quite right.

After a time, I realized that she did not want anything to do with my family. Well, none of that sat well with me or the family. We tried to accommodate her, but it could not be done. But like the rest of my life, I was being protected by God and loving people in the spirit world.

I tell you this story because there are mystical and spiritual things going on within this story that teach us a lot about ourselves, the interaction between the spirit world and the physical world, and how in the looking back over the path of our lives we will see the fingerprints of God himself, even in little details.

In this case, I got direct unmistakable feedback from Marilyn. She told me on three separate occasions in no uncertain words, "Do not stay with her." This mystical experience happened once when I was meditating and twice when I was sitting on my couch in the retreat with my mind quite blank, not thinking of anything in particular. Marilyn's voice was loud and clear and had a big sense of urgency to it. When I heard her words, I did not see an image of Marilyn but just heard what she said. She certainly was warning me to dump Megan. All three times, her words just came out of the blue. I was not expecting to have a mystical experience. I was not praying or anything like that. Her words just came to me very clearly and loudly. But it wasn't quite like this. I did not hear English words. Rather, it was more of a telepathic communication with tonal quality and accent of Marilyn. I also felt the strong presence of Marilyn in the room with me. So the best way to describe these encounters was that Marilyn was communicating with me telepathically with her unique vocal characteristics yet with no words being spoken. Her meaning was, however, unmistakable. And I heard with my mind everything she said to me.

We broke up shortly after that. I felt relief. At the time, I knew why. Shortly after I was told to stop seeing Megan, she got very angry at me for not manipulating my children the way she wanted. Well, to hell with that. I told her I would never live with anyone who had the potential for that level of rage inside them. So what was happening between the lines regarding this episode in my life? What was happening in the spirit world while I was living all this on earth? Lots.

The lesson here is that we all need to listen to those little positive loving inklings and urgings and act accordingly after praying for guidance from God. You will not hear trumpets blaring or someone speaking clear English to you, but you will get feelings, wonderments, and wordless communications to your heart about things. In my case, I heard plain English from Marilyn. That is unusual.

To profit from heavenly guidance, you need to practice meditation and prayer in a quiet place to really hear what your loved ones in heaven are trying to tell you. You need to make spiritual practice a daily exercise to hear God's loving voice in your life. Pay attention because someone in the spirit world who loves you may be trying to help you avoid something bad or turn you toward something good. But again, always pray to God for guidance first. Spiritual visits are not restricted to only when you meditate. But meditation sets the stage by opening up your heart to allow divine visits to happen when the spirit world wants them to. They are in control of the timing, not you or me.

After Megan and I broke up, God sent a rare diamond into my life. I love her with all my heart, and I know she loves me for who I am and how devoted I am to her. She is the woman I want to spend the rest of my life with. She has a heart of gold, and all I want is to make the rest of her days on the earth as enjoyable as possible. She is the one. She is everything I want in a companion, and I hope to spend the rest of my life together with this great woman. And yes, my family likes her a lot too.

God knows I cannot live alone, and I know He has been successful in working behind the scenes to see I meet just the right person to be with. Which spirits have helped me, I do not know, but I do know that there is no ego in heaven like on earth. Those in the spirit world want only what is good for us. They will work to help us find that special person who will make us happy if we are genuinely open to heavenly guidance. I know that Marilyn has been active in helping me find my life companion out of all the noise we have to go through dating lots of toads. In my case I went on countless coffee dates. My shortest date lasted about five minutes and I just had to get the hell out of there for that woman was awful.

But the good news is that I have met the one special woman that I will spend the rest of my life with. Her name is Evangeline. It means "bringer of good news." How wonderful is that. On our side of the veil, it always boils down to just how open our minds and hearts are to divine guidance from above. Then good things can happen. I did get guidance from the spirit world including Marilyn to bring meeting Evangeline to happen.

The moral of this story is that your loved ones in heaven do know very much what you are doing here on earth and the trials and tribulations you are going through. My children are happy again, and we remain a close-knit family sharing our lives together. As a widower, I cannot emphasize enough how precious that is.

What Did God Reveal of Himself?

1. The spirit world where our loved ones who have passed away is fully aware of what we are doing here and wants so much to help us succeed in our earthly mission. Lots of stuff goes on behind the spiritual scenes that we do not perceive, all of which is for our benefit

2. They do want to help us and try to communicate with us and nudge us in the right direction. In some cases, like me, our loved one needs to talk in plain telepathic English to get our attention.

3. It is up to us to take the time and effort to develop our mediation and prayer skills so that we will be able to hear not only our loving Father himself but also our beloved ones who have already passed over to the other side. They do want to help us, but it seems we are so busy with our lives that we never seem to have time to really meditate and pray.

4. Also, what I have just said just seems too good to be true. So most people ignore the possibility that what I have just said is true. Take my word for it. I speak from experience, and it is true. Believe it. It is the way creation works.

5. People who live close to God and the spirit world are still human, have human faults, and make mistakes just like everyone else. But the divine spirit world cares about what happens to us and will help us if we are attuned to them.

CHAPTER 9

My Multiple Visits to Heaven

Your Spirit Guides Are Real

*T*he following stories involve my spirit guide, Martin; my late wife; and other spirit beings that I could not identify but was aware of. I had no idea that these mystical events would happen in my life, but they did with great clarity. I am very blessed and humbled that God allowed me to experience what I am about to tell you. Basically, I was taken on multiple guided tours of a tiny slice of heaven in a home that is being prepared for me.

I must say that these stories of my travels in heaven in no way make me somehow better or above anyone else on this planet. I feel very privileged, honored, and humbled that I was allowed to see just a tiny part of heaven. I know for certain that heaven is infinite, and what I am going to describe to you is a very small sliver of the divine realm. I cannot stress enough that I am no different from you or anyone else. It is just that for reasons that I do not know or understand, God has allowed me to go out of my body and visit part of His divine realm and interact with the indescribable beauty, peace, and love that exists there.

This first story starts one day that I was feeling simply rotten. It had been only a few months since my wife died. I was horribly depressed. I had been fighting very strong urges to cry my eyes out, complete with dry heaves, which would then trigger bad asthma problems. I would wring my sweaty hands, and my anxiety levels would skyrocket through the roof. I had already cried from grief three times that day and was completely exhausted that evening. Emotions can really take your energy away. During this time in my life, my routine was to wake up, realize my wife was dead, try to make my coffee without crying my eyes out, which I never succeeded at, and then try to make it through the very long day, hiding from my kids and friends how in shambles my emotions were. I was a complete wreck in so many ways.

There is only one person on the planet who was visiting me that day. I have known her for over thirty years, and she is one of the greatest blessings I have in my life. We can say anything to each other as we share a deep friendship. She saw me break down that afternoon and can explain how I got the scars on my upper arms. She saw what happened. She is my dearest friend who was there for me when I desperately needed her.

After my dear friend left for home, it became evening, and the sun had gone down already. I went into Marilyn's room to sit on the recliner chair at the foot of her bed, the same bed where she passed away and the same recliner chair that I had spent so much time in staying close to her. I cleared my mind as best I could and prayed to God for healing and gave gratitude for all he has already done for me. I could already sense the presence of my two spirit guides in the room with me. It's much like the feeling you get when you can feel a loved one in the room with you. It is like there is a certain positive energy there that has a personality and is focused on your well-being. There were a few times before this where I could see Martin, but not this time. Then I started to talk to Martin and Randal, my two guides at the time. I asked him a simple question. I said with my mind, "Martin, what is my wife doing now?"

He instantly answered me by saying this, "She is preparing a place for you." Well, this is something I certainly did not expect. Actually,

I expected nothing in return, but to get an answer like this was very surprising. His answer was very clear, and there was no doubt that it was not my imagination playing tricks on me. I never anticipated what he said.

Mystical answers are almost always short and very much to the point.

I then asked Martin, "What do you mean? How?" Martin did not answer with a thought this time. Rather, he showed me a vision of what she was doing. But this vision had all the feelings that I was really there where my wife was. It was not like I was watching TV or a movie, for example. I had no perception of my body and lost all awareness that I was at home in the recliner chair. I got the strong feeling that I was really there in heaven seeing her for the first time since she had passed away. I was instantly out of my body in a manner I do not understand. I could see not only my wife but also the surroundings. For all intents and purposes, I was somehow instantly in heaven with my wife watching her and what she was doing. This mystical event was not like the one I had on the cruise ship the year before. I never got any feeling of instant travel to another place or any kind of acceleration or going through a portal or anything we might connect with traveling somewhere. I was just instantly in the place where she was, and I was watching her.

She was dressed in a white robe. I could see her as if I were about fifty feet away. I saw her long black hair the way she wore it the first time we met in graduate school. She was planting flowers in a garden in front of what I took to be a house. I have to say this was the most beautiful sight I had ever seen in my life. The light seemed like it came from everywhere. There were no shadows. The garden was terraced leading up to the house, which was on top. A paved pathway led from where I was standing around to the right and up to the house. This house is something like I have never seen before. It glistened in the light. It seemed to be made of beautiful marble and clear crystal. The crystal sparkled in the light against what was a blue sky.

Beautiful mountains were in the background. The structure of the house contained crystal spires reaching up into the sky and was surrounded with the most beautiful gardens I have ever seen. Marilyn always loved flowers and was always tending to our garden around our house. She continues to love flowers and was doing something she loved. How appropriate. Then after a very short time, the visit was over. I regained perceptions of my body and the room I was in. I thanked Martin for showing me this. I lost my focus, and my mind started to cloud over with other thoughts. So I ended my meditation with a prayer and felt better for the experience.

I went away from this unexpected mystical experience with a deep contentment that I actually saw that she was doing great and engaged in activities that she loved. But immediately afterward, I realized that I wanted more. I wanted to speak with my wife now that I knew she was okay, and I wanted to know much more about this part of heaven she was in. I wanted to know more about this house she was planting flowers around. But for now, I was very content that I was given this much by God and ever so thankful that I was allowed to see a part of heaven. I slept better that night. This was a rare treat for me.

Heaven Is Real

After a while, I began to realize that we all started in a heavenly place. Those who live good lives and put the love of God and His will above all else will go back to heaven. Leading a good life is very important, but everyone must also accept that Jesus Christ is our Lord. I have come to believe that the best single and overwhelming prayer to God is the prayer of how you live your life. It needs to be according to the teachings of Jesus.

Remember that Jesus is the way, the truth, and the light. We all started in the heavenly realm before we came to earth to experience and learn what the physical realm has to teach us. When we pass back into the heavenly realm after leading a godly life, the circle is completed. We are back where we started but changed profoundly. And when we return, we may enjoy more of God's infinite creation by means of what we have learned and experienced on this earth. This is what God promised us in the beginning. It is what I described in the very first part of this book.

In my spiritual life, I once thought that in order to get a glimpse of heaven, you needed to have a near-death experience. The work conducted by Dr. Raymond Moody more than twenty years ago focused on this, with people who were clinically dead but brought back with modern medical methods. He documented what they experienced and published books on the subject. This was my first exposure to the thought that people could visit heaven and return to the physical realm. But I thought that you needed to almost die to do that.

I was to find out that one did not need to almost die to visit heaven. I was to find out that God, in His infinite love for us and His grace, allows a person to visit heaven in a limited manner through prayer and deep meditation. But it is God who decides if you are to be allowed within the heavenly realm. At least for me, I cannot will myself there. I believe that no one can will that on their own. God must allow it. There is a veil that separates heaven from Earth. There are many good reasons for this. But there is one thing that flows freely through the veil, and that is love. This was just my first visit into the heavenly realm. There are others that I will tell you about. They came unexpectedly, and all were different, containing new information about heaven, my late wife, and the house I saw on top of the hill with the beautiful gardens.

I pray that this story about what I have experienced brings peace and joy into your heart and increases your understanding of what happens during passing away and afterward. Remember the following: "Death is the gate of life." (St. Bernard of Clairvaux).

It seemed so very simple to ask a request of Martin, my spirit guide, and see my darling wife and instantly where I was in heaven close by her. I was indeed in heaven, and my physical body was nowhere to be found, sensed, or perceived. This says many things regarding God and how much he loves his children. God loves His children so very much that at the right time in my life after Marilyn passed away, He led me to a wonderful woman whom I have grown to love deeply and will spend the rest of my life with. I continue to relearn the same lesson over and over again. Good things will come to those who put God first in their lives according to His perfect timing, not according to ours. In my case, it seems that I always get to the end of my rope before God answers my needs and prayers. I was about to give up completely looking for a partner to share my life with. It was during my last gasp, so to speak, when I met the woman who brings good news. She is the answer to my needs, wishes, prayers, and yearnings. I look forward now to the future sharing our lives together in love, peace, and harmony. I also know that Marilyn definitely approves of my darling life partner. For me, what God has brought forth in my life through my sweetie cannot get any better. I just wish I would have met her sooner. But then, we all must remember that God's timing is perfect, and mine certainly is not.

More Visits to Heaven

For reasons unknown to me, God allowed me multiple trips out of my body across the veil into the heavenly realm. I can only assume that these visits are an anointed part of my spiritual journey here on earth, and God wants me to tell His other children about what I experience. This will strengthen faith and help those who read this on their own spiritual journeys. Now, during these mystical visits, I did not experience the fullness of heaven or feel the extent of the intense divine love that someone who is totally in spirit with no remaining connection to the physical realm would feel. They have passed to the other side completely, but I only got a tiny taste of heaven. Yet, it still was an overwhelming love- and peace-filled experience to be there. I do not claim to be an expert but rather a person who has experienced something wonderful and am humbled by it all.

With that in mind, what I did experience was something that is beautifully unforgettable and life-changing and will always bring a consolation into my heart for being separated from my wife. I have to emphasize that what I am about to tell you are things that are very real. During these visits, I had no idea what was going to happen next. I was surprised by so many things that I never knew existed, and I can remember every detail even though all this happened years ago. All three of the above characteristics are hallmarks of a real mystical experience, not a dream or some kind or hallucination. If there is any doubt in my mind, I would never write about it. It would be an absolute horrific sin to modify the telling of anything divine I experienced.

There were a number of times I went to heaven, with Marilyn leading the way for me. These events happened during deep meditation sessions where I lost all sensation of being on earth or in my body. Martin, my spirit guide, and other spirit beings always were with us during these visits. I cannot thank God enough to allow me to see a tiny portion of heaven and not just experience a vision. It would be arrogant of me to claim that I saw heaven, implying that I saw the whole thing. I know that I did not, but rather some small portion of divine paradise. These visits were the real thing, and I was indeed out of my body and actually interacting with the divine beings I name here. What a blessing I have had for a lifetime.

After I saw Marilyn on my first visit, digging flowers in front of a magnificent house made of crystal and marble, I got the impression that the house she was gardening in front of was going to be the house I was going to live in once I cross over. Over a period of time, I got more curious about what the inside looked like. The outside was the most beautiful home that anyone on earth can imagine. It stood on top of a hill with greenery, flowers, a few trees, and other shrubs surrounding it. There were beautiful walkways that went around the house with many plants that had wonderfully colored flowers I have never seen before. Many of them had colors I have never seen either. The home overlooked a valley that had a stream running through it. Other homes were scattered around this valley among the trees.

The one thing I noticed was that there were no shadows on the ground. Light was coming from everywhere. There were no shadows at all. I could hear birds singing but no insects to bother you. The sky was blue with the whitest of puffy clouds scattered around the sky.

Tall mountains stood in the distance. Some of them had snow on their peaks. All the colors were so vivid and nothing like nothing I have ever seen on earth.

Somehow, my second visit began at the bottom steps leading up to the front entrance of the house on the hill. The marble was white with a beautiful meandering pattern to it. I would say there were approximately twenty steps in all that led to the final level where you could then pass through the front entrance and into the house. Two very large Greco-Roman columns were at either side of the top level of the steps. The first thing I noticed as I got to the top level of the steps was that the front entrance did not have any doors. In fact, I found out later after walking throughout this fabulous home that there were no doors anywhere. This house did not have any doors at all. After I thought about it, I realized that in heaven there is no need for doors. What is there that you could possibly want to keep out? The answer is nothing. Nobody is going to steal anything. And as for the need for privacy, that is accomplished in other ways, which I was soon to discover. The walls of this home were transparent from the inside. You could see out, but I do not remember being able to see in from the outside.

As I passed through the entrance portal to the inside of the house, I was absolutely shocked. The inside of the house appeared to be at least ten times larger than the outside of the house would indicate. How could this be? The inside of the house was plainly huge with walls made out of something like transparent crystal.

As I walked into this house, I realized that this home took on the ambience of not only a home but also a personalized cathedral. Not only were the walls made of quartzlike substance but also the roof. There was a main hallway, which connected the entrance of the house all the way to the rear. It ran through the center of this home. On both sides of this main hallway were separate areas that could be seen from the main hallway, but they were about eight steps lower than the main hallway. Each separate area had its own separate entrance.

The hallway was defined by what I will call marble planters with gorgeous flowers growing in each of them. And it is these planters that separated the different areas of this home. Everything in this home that was made of this marblelike substance had a translucent quality to it, and the patterns inlaid into the marble all had different varieties of earth tones. It was absolutely gorgeous. It had the quiet of a library. Yet at the same time, I could feel the life that existed within this home. There was a peaceful vibrancy to the energy that I sensed within this immaculate home. About twenty or thirty steps from the doorless entrance, I turned to my left, and there was an entrance to the first separate area, which was about eight steps down from the main hallway.

As I turned left and walked into this entrance, which was again defined by gorgeous planters with beautiful flowers, I again turned left and proceeded down the eight or ten steps into an area that turned out to be shaped like a little cove. It was an area of communing with the Blessed Virgin Mary. All I could make out from this area was a statue of the Blessed Virgin Mary inside this alcove and very comfortable seats where a person could rest comfortably, contemplate, and pray.

The feeling I got while in this area was almost as if the Blessed Virgin Mary were present there. One can feel her love gently and warmly surrounding anyone who came into this alcove of prayer to her and with her. The warmth and love there is a wonderful experience to have being there. It goes beyond words trying to describe this place of worship and prayer inside this home. I walked back up the stairs and proceeded down the main hallway toward the rear of this marvelous home. As I moved around in this home, Marilyn was always behind my left shoulder. It is interesting that when she was here on earth, she would always walk with me behind my left shoulder. Some things never change, I guess.

The next area I encountered on the left was a library. My perceptions in this area are limited, but I did find many books there.

But these were not ordinary books. I opened a large book and set it on a reading table. When I leafed through the pages, I realized that these pages contained pictures and some text, but the pictures were not stationary. They were alive. I instantly knew that this was a history book that depicted various events in human history, and I also was given to know that if I wanted to, I could literally enter into the scenes depicted.

For example, there was a picture of Columbus stepping off a small boat on the beach of a tropical island, and if I wanted to, I could have stepped into that picture and be there with him at that time to experience precisely what happened during that event. I remembered that time and distance in heaven has no real meaning, and it is these qualities of heaven that allow heavenly spirits to experience so many different events in human history just by entering into the scene. I was unable to perceive how many different books were in this library, but there were two comfortable seats where one could sit down and explore in a timeless way more of human history and other parts of God's creation.

Just think about this. There are books that are alive with the real events of history available for you to enter into what is depicted so you can experience it firsthand. You are literally there among whatever is shown in the pictures of these books. I never would have thought this was possible. But in God's creation, there are infinite possibilities for all of us to explore and learn. The laws of physics that we experience here on earth just do not matter in heaven. We are not restricted there as we are here. What a wonderful thing to know and look forward to.

The next area on the left side of the main hallway was eight to ten steps down from the main hallway like all the other areas. As I entered this area, I could see that it was larger and was intended to be a social area, a gathering place for friends, family, and other loved ones to congregate and enjoy each. Here you could enjoy their experiences and deeply connect with one another in the divine matrix of life that God has created. I could only imagine the parties and other gatherings that could take place there. But for now, there was only me, Marilyn, and our spirit guides.

There was a fourth area on the left side of the hallway, but I could not perceive what it was. I did still have limitations to what I could perceive because I had not yet passed over to this side of creation. I then arrived at the rear of this wondrous home, and there was a huge balcony outside, which overlooked an absolutely gorgeous valley below. Yes, there were trees and other kinds of things that you would find in a forest on earth, but it was just so much more magnificently beautiful with trees and other plants that I had never seen before. In the distance, there was a gorgeous mountain range, and the peaks of the mountains were capped with snow. And these peaks kissed the blue sky above. It was a different kind of blue from what we see here.

The entire landscape seemed alive, and it seemed to project a love for all who lived there among its forested areas, mountains, and valleys. I got the feeling that there was not one square inch where there was not intense love of all that was alive with vibrant color, and everything there sang its own songs of worship to God while also loving all that entered into this magnificent paradise. Oh, dear reader, I wish words would do justice to what I experienced there.

On the right side of the main hallway were also several areas that were accessible by steps downward leading to them. There was one very special area that could not be seen from the hallway. This area was very private. It was designed for two spirits to be intimate with each other when they chose to do so. If you have ever wondered whether there is sex in heaven, the answer is no, not like here on earth.

The intimate and loving intermingling of spirits on earth is very crude and primitive in comparison to what happens in heaven. In heaven, it is far more dignified and intense. The only way I can describe this is what Marilyn showed me. In spirit form, a person can merge with another person. When this happens, the two become one, each experiencing the uniqueness of the other's love. Each of our personalities and the unique fingerprints of our heartfelt love are different for all others of God's children. No two loves are the same, just as no two spirit beings are the same. It is the perception of our individual loves that make us unique and serve to bring about our personal identity. The intimate merging of two loving beings strengthens the loving bonds they share together. This intimate merging into one allows each person to become temporarily one with each other, and each can experience directly the deepest emotions and love of the other.

This results in an ecstasy that can be experienced only by those who deeply love and are in spirit form and in heaven. I only got the slightest taste of this while I was there. This coming together of two into one is very holy, divine, magnificently dignified, and loving beyond words. I wanted to stay there for an extremely long time, but Marilyn said that there were other things I needed to see first.

Another area on the right side of the hallway was something very special just for me. My late wife told me that she knew how much I enjoy exploring the universe. She arranged for me a telescope inside this home. It was pointing outward through the perfectly transparent windows. She told me that there is nothing in the universe that I could not see with this telescope. What a wonderful gift that awaits me. Just imagine that I will have my own personal telescope that is far more powerful than anything that exists on earth or put into space. What a wonderful gift this is for me.

The final area that I saw on the right side of the home was another worship alcove. As I stepped down into this area, I could see that this was an area for prayer to the Holy Trinity. Again, I could feel the lightness, warmth, and love that existed throughout this part of the home. The character of this cove was different, yet all-consuming, bright, and wonderfully fulfilling, which gave a sense of total belonging where there was no separation between God and me. A person could spend an infinite amount of time here and ask questions of God, and there would be answers. But during this visit, I was not able to ask God any questions.

This ended my familiarization with this heavenly home. But before I lost my meditative focus, I also saw a second level to this home, which also was on the sides along the windows. I noted also that although we could see perfectly outside from the inside, one could not be outside and see was going on inside. I look forward one day to going back there and seeing all this in more detail. This heavenly home on top of the small hill surrounded by gorgeous terraced gardens full of flowers, each of which seemed to sing its personal songs of love, is apparently going to be my home in heaven when my time comes. This is such a delicious experience to look forward to.

There is one more thing that I want to point out. This home was not constructed like you would think it would be. I was given to know that there were no workman, there were no blueprints, and there was nobody hauling the quartz and setting it into place. This home was literally thought into existence. How this happens, I do not know. But I can say with certainty this home was indeed literally thought into existence. At this point, I do not know whose thoughts it was, but nonetheless, that is the way things happen in heaven. I do believe that it was Marilyn, though, but I have no proof, and she was not saying anything about that. In heaven, thoughts are manifested into reality. Think about all the power thoughts have in heaven; it is the power to create just by thinking something into existence.

I think there is a lesson to be learned that applies here on earth. Each person's thoughts on earth can become habits of thinking. Habits of thinking can become a person's character. A person's character then can become their personality. This personality then interacts with the physical realm, and this interaction then manifests itself into consequences that are played out in this physical realm. So be careful of what you think, for you ultimately will enjoy the results or suffer the consequences.

The Gates of Heaven

In my life, I have come to realize that the appearance of heaven may be different for different people. It is like seeing the same thing from different angles. I think that heaven, and for that matter, other spiritual realities, modify their appearance to conform to the expectations we have built up over the years based on what we were taught or on our life experiences and beliefs. But in all cases, heaven exceeds the joy, beauty, and outright majesty that we may imagine in our minds. In my case, one afternoon, I did my usual meditation practice focusing on just what the gates of heaven were really like. I was amazed at what happened next—and that is an understatement.

During this particular meditation, I became very deep within it. I again lost all sense of being on earth, and my reality became the spiritual realm again. As I did consciously focus on the gates of heaven, I found myself on a road. In the distance, I did see wonderful light, heavenly light of love and peace. I somehow again was not in my body. I was not in another body, either. Rather, I was formless. I had no legs or other body parts we normally think of. To say that I walked up the path toward the gate would be a misnomer. Instead, I traveled up this path that led to the gates of heaven. There were beautiful clouds all around me. The path I was on appeared to be somehow suspended among the gorgeous clouds of blue and white. But it felt solid, even though I did not have a body. I cannot explain this.

As I traveled closer and closer to the gate, I began to perceive that it was made of translucent gold. It had beautiful pillars that stood about twenty feet high. The gate between the pillars was darker and looked like what we would call wrought iron, but it was not iron. It was very decorative. Getting closer still, I saw two figures standing on either side of the gate. I initially thought that one of them must be St. Peter. But I was to find out soon that St. Peter was not one of them. To my great surprise, and once I got close enough to see the faces of the two figures standing at the gate, I was shocked. I had no idea this would happen. Those two figures I saw were people I knew who had passed away years before.

To my astonishment, they were my dear Grandpa Troha and Uncle Bill. They were on my mother's side of the family. Both of these people I loved very much. I felt so very loved and comfortable with them when I would visit my grandparents' home in Savannah, Illinois.

When I got close enough to the gate, both of my dear ancestors had big smiles for me. My grandpa looked much younger than I remember him, and so did my uncle. Somehow unknown to me, they knew that I wanted to see the gates of heaven, and they appeared to me that way. Somehow, they knew what I was thinking and what I needed to see, and in their own personal love, they made that happen for me. This experience I had points to just how close the spiritual realm is to our inner being and inner selves. What we think is somehow known in heaven. Think about that and all its ramifications. I find this to be such a wondrous and reassuring thing to realize. When you hear someone say that you are never alone, it is so very true. What you are experiencing now and your thoughts are always known by God and others in the heavenly realm. Why? Because you are an inexorable part of the divine matrix or brotherhood of God's children.

What Did God Reveal of Himself?

1. Intensely loving another person and being loyal to that person may allow us to visit him or her while he or she is in heaven, and we are allowed to pass through the veil into the heavenly realm if we have enough faith and love and an open mind. In my case, I was allowed to see my wife from a distance doing the things she loved to do. I was allowed to see this astonishing home and be guided by Marilyn, who gave me such wonderful information about heaven.

2. In later communications, when Marilyn would come to earth to see me, she would be wearing much different clothing from the first time I saw her. The first time I saw her in her new clothes, I thought she was the most beautiful woman in the whole universe. It seems that, just like earth, there is nothing static in heaven, except that God is infinite and unchanging. You get to choose what you wear. God wants us to grow in our spirit, even while we are in heaven. I have come to understand from these experiences that there is no end to how far we can

grow in the spirit, going higher and higher in the deepness of love and closeness to God our Father. I have perceived this with Marilyn. Over the years, her appearance has changed to be more translucent, more ephemeral, and beautiful. The clothes she wears are no longer the simple white robe she was wearing the first time I saw her. As I write this, her clothing is really beyond description other than to say that her "dress" is an intermingling of gorgeous translucent pastels that defy proper description.

3. God does allow different people to actually visit heaven when a loved one is there. This happened to me multiple times. The next chapter describes what happened during my subsequent visits.

4. When we go to heaven, we keep our personality. We do not play harps and float on clouds and stuff like that. Based on being with Marilyn in heaven, the times I was with her, and how she talks with me here on earth, I can say that she definitely has the same personality. But she has a much larger perspective on things and is in a better position to advise me on the best things to do and what to avoid.

5. Something that is unexpected is one of the markers of a true mystical experience. If we are told something unexpected or something we never heard before, we can be sure that it is not our memory or imagination working. Rather, it is a mystical source interacting with us.

6. Heaven is beyond wonderful imagination. I could never have guessed the things I saw and experienced there. And I only saw such a small part of all God created for His children.

CHAPTER 10

The Physical Realm Meets the Spiritual Realm

Changing Clothes

S ince my wife's death, God has blessed me with an enormous gift of being able to see and sometimes hear the spirit beings that are close to me: my spirit guides, Martin, Randal, and Alliachwalla. As I write this, it has been almost five years since Marilyn passed away, and over that time, I have been graciously blessed by God to see her many times. Again, one of the very interesting things about spiritual vision is that you do not have to turn your head to see any spirits around you. Your eyes do not have to be open either. You merely have to adjust your attention and focus to the different areas surrounding you, and you will then see what is there. It is not like using your eyes, though. It is quite different for me. I can see the shapes, outlines, colors of clothing, and some details of the visiting beings. My spiritual acuity varies from time to time, from being quite detailed to vague and what we would call out of focus. One time I saw Randal wearing a derby hat complete with mustache and English-looking clothes. He told me he was from a small town north of London. I wondered if he liked tea and crumpets.

Over these last years, I have seen Marilyn change her appearance. For the first few months, I would always see her in a beautiful, full-length white robe. But then later on I would see her in beautiful skirts and blouses, but I could not, for some reason, see her feet. After a while, she seemed to have settled on various white blouses and the most beautiful blue skirts that go down slightly below the knee. One of her favorite blouses is a white one with a deep V-neck. Many times, but not always, she would wear a gorgeous diamond necklace that would fill the V of the blouse. And I would see her wearing a gorgeous diamond ring I first saw when she extended her hand to me from above about a month after she passed away. Her black hair is always very beautiful. Everything that I can see in detail is more beautiful than here on earth.

Me and my big mouth. She always did love jewelry. But I noticed over a long period of time that she would always appear to me in a white blouse and a blue skirt. One evening when she appeared to be that way, I teased her and said, "Gee, I think you are in a fashion rut. All I ever see you in is a white blouse and blue skirt. What's with that?" She responded by saying, "Well, how do you like this?" And with that response, I instantly saw her in a red negligee with puffy black trim that looked like something you would find in a bordello. I became both shocked and embarrassed. Now, this is my late wife for you. If she were here on earth, she would probably do the same thing if I had said something like that. Some things just don't change. Once I saw her in that red bordello suit, I said, "It's okay". Thank you, sweetheart, but I think I like the blue skirt and white blouse far better." And then again, instantly she changed her appearance back to the way it was. I would have never guessed that spirit beings could change appearances so quickly.

Over the years, other things have changed with Marilyn's appearance. When I first saw her standing behind my right shoulder a few months after she passed away, her hairdo was much the same as it was when she was first diagnosed with cancer. Her facial features were also identical, except that she appeared much younger than she was during those last few years of her life. I am told by other credible spiritual sources who write about spiritual matters that everybody in heaven is thirty years old. It is only Jesus Christ who is thirty-three, which symbolizes authority and rank over God's other children.

In more recent times, my wife's general appearance has evolved into more gossamer, more transparent, and flowing. I cannot see her in as much detail as before. Nonetheless, it is certain that it is her for I recognize her energy and personality. That does not change.

What Did God Reveal of Himself?

1. The physical realm in which we all live in is closely intertwined with the spiritual realm. They are not as separate as almost all people think. In many ways, I have come to believe that they tend to overlap. The spiritual world is accessible to us. The important caution I would give to anyone seeking the spirit world is to pray to God for guidance. Make sure that Jesus Christ is your savior and protector and direct your prayers to only our Heavenly Father and Jesus Christ. There are evil spirits out there, and they can and will deceive you if you stray from our loving God. This is serious business, and never discount the power behind spirit beings. If you do not pray to God in the name of Jesus Christ and if you try to communicate with spirit beings, you never know what you will get.

2. It is intense love that flows through the veil that separates heaven from this world. It flows freely as the only thing that does so. But if you deeply love someone who has passed to the other side, ask God for His protection and guidance first. Then ask God if you may see and interact with your departed loved one. If this does not work the first time, and it usually does not, be sure to open your heart and mind to our Heavenly Father in the name of Jesus Christ. It is permissible to bug God,

as I do, regarding your request. Then wait. Your answer may come in a different form than experiencing your loved one as I have. It all depends on how God thinks it is best for you. My experiences with my departed wife are testimony that all this is possible. I should also say that this story is only one of the very many times communicating with my wife has happened.

3. Usually, each person on earth has one spirit guide or guardian angel. In my case, I have had one and sometimes as many as three with two angels for protection during my very vulnerable moments, especially right Marilyn's death. God does likewise for all his children, I believe. It is just that most people do not open themselves to perceiving what God is doing for them, especially during times of trauma and agony. Perhaps I needed so many guides and angels because I really needed the help where others do not need as much. I do not know. I can imagine God telling his angels, "Well, we all know Rich is a basket case. Please get down there again and see what you can do for him." I think of myself as spiritually strong, but in reality, maybe I'm not as strong as I think. But I do rely on what God told me years ago—that I am among his best. I cherish this thought more than anything else on this planet.

CHAPTER 11

A Deep Conversation with God Our Father

Complaining to God

*I*f you are like most people, including me, you pray and feel it is a one-way conversation. You pray to God for what you need, tell our Father of your love for Him, or give Him thanks for the blessings you perceive in life. But God does not answer. He remains silent, and it is as if you were talking to the wall—no response. Boy, can this be frustrating. In this respect, I am just like you. However, even if you get no response, I believe He hears every prayer that you ever have said. We all have to remember that God talks silently.

God communicates to us in subtle ways. It can be telepathic or through feelings or through something someone said that just rings a bell in your mind. In one case for me, a hummingbird approached me and hovered about two feet in front of my face for about a minute. This was when I was laying down in my recliner on the patio. Previous to that, I was asking God if He really cared to even listen to my prayers. The hummingbird was His answer. And the answer was an emphatic *yes*. It was such a strange yet warm feeling to have a beautiful hummingbird choose that exact moment to hover right in front of me for so long just looking at me. It was quite an experience for those who pay attention but for those without an open mind, they will never notice God trying to communicate.

But on occasion, in my case, I have had conversations with God himself. Yes, I have. And I must emphasize that it was or is not a figment of my imagination. I actually established direct one-on-one communication with God our Father, and we had quite a conversation. God and I have had multiple conversations over the past years. The one that I want to tell you about is the time I was complaining bitterly to God for all the shit that has happened in my life and how miserable I was after Marilyn died. I was very angry with God. By the way, you can get angry with God. He has heard it all, so nothing you can say will be new to Him. There was a time that I could spit fire. I was so upset and angry with life, with God, and with everything in my horrific, trauma-filled life. This was about two years after Marilyn died.

I remained devastated and needed sedatives and other medications to cope with life as a widower. Intense trauma was the order of the day. I had horrible bodily sensations and sometimes lost control of my sobbing over my devastating loss. I could not stand the pain during the flashbacks. I went through grief counseling for one year, and that seemed to help a little bit. The counselor was a good one and did understand what I was going through. Talking about things does help. Needless to say, my wife's death greatly affected my prayer life and the content of my meditations. That is when I could calm down enough to pray and meditate. These times were few and far between.

After a while, I had already heard all the well-intentioned explanations about why my wife passed away when she did. Frankly, all of them seemed too packaged in standard theological or philosophical blather. After a while of hearing all the explanations that she is in heaven, that it was meant to be this way, and that I should be thankful that she was not suffering anymore, I was ready to explode. I sincerely thank everyone who was trying to help me cope with my situation, but I quickly realized that there was no one on this planet who could really help me crawl out of the deep emotional hole I was in. Nobody had *the* answer. I descended into a very deep depression that held a strong grip on every waking moment I had in this life. I realized after a long time that I should not expect anyone to have the answer, for death is part of life and is unavoidable. But why should she have been struck down with a painful illness only to pass away and leave me behind—and at such a young age? I awoke each morning when the weight of a mallet would strike a crushing blow to my head and heart. The realization in those few seconds of being a widower would hit me like thunder, which would start the day that I hoped I would survive. My guts would then started to churn, my head would start aching, and my energy would quickly evaporate. There I would lay in bed wondering just how I could make it through the day. I came to believe the saying that for those who chose to truly love others will certainly experience suffering and agony. And so it was with me.

I was also angry at God. Even though I was angry with God, I knew these things happened every day to people, and I never asked God, "Why Marilyn and me?" I felt betrayed by God allowing this to happen to us and my whole family. But I never really did ask, "Why me?" There is so much suffering in this world it would be foolish even to ask the question.

Yes, I Talk Directly to God our Father

But as God seems to do, even with my terrible attitude, I was about to find out how immeasurably loving and loyal God is even in times like this. I was going to find out that God is never disturbed by our anger at him or our bad attitudes. For me, having a bad attitude should have been more inexcusable since, a year earlier, I completed my master's degree program in pastoral ministry. But this did not faze our Father one little bit. I was to find out that all he had for me was pure and intense love. I was about to have another divine mystical experience. I could sense it coming directly to me. This time, it was a direct communication with God our Father Himself. Yes, God did unexpectedly communicate with me during a deep meditation session I had about eighteen months after Marilyn's passing.

My unexpected mystical experience started as all my meditations do. I sat down in my prayer chair, put my ear buds in, started some meditation music on very softly, put my soundproof earmuffs on, and adjusted the chair and headrest for maximum comfort. I then started to clear my mind and started to say my mantra to our Lord and Father. When I was in a deep meditative state of mind, I started to talk to God not in English but rather in feelings and emotions. You can offer up to God non-English feelings without words as a very effective way to communicate to our Creator. Most people do not know that, but I like doing that.

After a while of praying like that, I started to see the dark void where many people before me have said "God lives." It is full of light but black. Yes, this is an oxymoronic phrase, but nonetheless, it is true. Eben Alexander has written about it in his book "Heaven Is Real". I suggest strongly you get a copy and read it.

Then it happened. I knew God became present for me to say anything I wanted to say to Him. Our Heavenly Father wanted to listen to what was on my mind. God did not say anything nor did I see him, but there was absolutely no doubt that He was present for me, and I could sense his love, peace, and eternal character. With that I said, "Father, why has all this pain and agony happened, and why did Marilyn have to die? I am in such horrible suffering, Father. Not a minute goes by in my life that is not filled with grievous loneliness, horrible sadness, no appetite with nausea no energy to even have a life worth living." Our Father God responded silently with words He said directly into my brain that I am one of "His best" or strongest representatives or emissaries on earth. He counts on me to take on the tough assignments when I come here to live. Well, I did not feel very "best" or strong at that moment, but that is what Father communicated to me.

Then God showed me a road that was really a timeline that

extended far into the past. It appeared as if I were standing in this road, and looking down it, I was actually looking into the past. It is as if distance were really time. The farther I looked down this road, the further back in time I was looking. At different spots on this road, there was a person standing on the edge of the road. I immediately remembered that the multiple people I was seeing were actually me at all the times I came to earth to do God's work in the past. Yes, I have been here many times. In the vision God showed me, the distances I saw were really time. God was showing me that this lifetime I was bitterly complaining about was just one of many times I have been here to do what needed to be done according to His will both for me and this world.

But being the spiritual hardhead I am, I complained strongly to our Father that I have always completely obeyed his wishes and have always put his tasks for me ahead of anything else in my lives in the past. "Couldn't you, Father, have granted me just once the need to save Marilyn's life?" God, again without words, acknowledged that and gave me the feeling that Marilyn was safe and happy and was in a position where she could help me the most from the spirit world while I was still here. If she stayed with me here on earth, that could not happen. There was an overarching reason for her leaving the earthly realm, and I would understand it more when I left here too. I did not have the balls to tell God that I missed Marilyn terribly and that I wanted her back. But the bottom line on this higher level conversation was that Marilyn would now be in a place where she could effectively help me complete my assignment here during my life. But that meant I needed to stay on earth while she went to heaven. Our not being together was the price to be paid. But the reality is that we are still together across the veil since she will be constantly helping me complete my purpose here on earth. Nonetheless, I felt that I got the short end of that deal. This conversation was one of two concurrent conversations I had with God that afternoon. Yes, there were two conversations with God happening at the same time.

More Than One Conversation at the Same Time

All the while, this conversation went on with me complaining, I began to realize that there was a second line of communication simultaneously going on between God and me. There was an underlying conversation going on underneath the more ordinary conversation I was having that I just described. It was deeper and more fundamental to my existence and relationship with Our Father in heaven. It was as if we were speaking to each other on two separate phone lines both at the same time. In this second line of communication, there were no words but only images and deep feelings of love and total familiarity between the both of us. The image I got was one of knowing that God and I have had a history together for at least millions of years.

This more fundamental conversation was as if we were one in spirit, totally committed to the same will, and expressing love for each other that has existed further back in time than I can perceive. My complaining was the superficial conversation. The more fundamental communication was filled with love and understanding between us. Yes, there was a blessed unity between God and me where we jointly and lovingly remembered past adventures I participated in according to God's will. God was ever so thankful for all that I have done in the previous eons and loves me more than can be described. I am one of those of His children who will do anything God asks of me but reserves the right to bitch and moan. I think God considers this side of me amusing. Ugh!

Yes, I know this sounds fantastic for someone who has not experienced this, but it is exactly what I experienced. I know most people have never heard words like this before. This is something new and profound. Also remember that Christian dogma states that God is both transcendent and infinite. Therefore, our understandings of God can never be complete. When we hear of something we never heard before, we must not throw it out of our minds into the "this-cannot-be-true" file. You will never learn more about God or draw closer to him by doing that. Take my last statement or leave it behind. It will depend on where you are in your personal spiritual journey. But I remain with what I said. I experienced this exactly as I said. God and I have had a very close relationship for a very, very long time, which spans multiple lifetimes going back into the very distant past.

In the spirit world, you can see things that are not visible in this physical world. During my communication with Our Father that afternoon, God showed me an image that I had always been outspoken to him as part of my nature, and my complaining was no different this time than many times in the distant past. Yet I always did His will, and He said He is very grateful for my love and loyalty to him. So while I was complaining, this other communication was also going on that showed how inexorably close I am to Him and that we have a very long history within creation together. Basically, I am His child who complains a lot, but then I do what God wants. He finds that lovable, according to the image of emotions He showed me across the eons. I was being shown this while I was complaining about my dear wife and losing her. God understands every little bit of me. He also understands every little bit of you, too. Remember this.

He did not tell me that my troubles would go away. Rather, I was led to believe that they would not. I would have to live through them just like everyone else. But this mystical experience during my meditation did bring relief to me and more strength to endure what life had brought me. It still stinks, but I know that in my existence I have been here before and lived through this kind of thing before. I will live through it this time, as well, even though at times it does not seem like it. I still think it sucks very badly and is horribly painful. I believe everyone on earth experiencing these kinds of things and has to live through them as I do. I am not special in any way regarding this. Life is life, and it is for everyone. But somehow I feel like Moses when he cried out to God, saying, "Just how much more do you demand of me?" I really do need a rest from everything that has happened.

What Did God Reveal of Himself?

1. We never know when God will make a personal appearance and communicate with us or bring us exactly what we need to endure what it is in our lives. But we must have the eyes to see, ears to hear, and an open mind to let God enter. If we ever think that God would not appear to little ol' me, then we just closed the door. Let us not do that! Let us let our minds be open to God.

2. Even though God may appear and be with us, it does not mean He is the Candy Man who will hand out all the goodies we want. In my case, over the years, that certainly has not been true. He has never said to me, "Rich, because you are so close to me, I will make things easier for you." Quite to the contrary, I am told by very spiritual people who know my life that things have been far harder for me than others. Well, it certainly feels like it.

3. God does not play favorites. Even though I feel I am very close to God, I still have all the same issues other people have. Look at the lives of the apostles. Also read about all the saints and what happened to them. All had very hard painful lives. We all have our crosses to bear in the name of Jesus Christ.

4. God has a myriad of ways that he uses to communicate with us. Each one is tailor-made to fit the situation at the time. God does meet us where we are spiritually. In other words, He will craft His communication so that we will understand and not be left wondering, "What was that?" Again, that is if we have an open mind.

5. God has individually and personally known us long before we came to earth and knows our personalities in great detail. Like the Bible says, God even knows the number of hairs on your head.

6. God does not hide things from us if we are open and able to understand. He showed me a road, which was actually a personal timeline that stretched back for untold years before I was born, and revealed to me just how close and personal our relationship has been throughout time.

7. God does not anger in my experience. He unconditionally loves each of us all the time no matter what our attitude is. I have a bad attitude at times, yet I know without any doubt that God loves me unconditionally and that I will do His will as best I can, even when I complain a lot and suffer. But I do feel that I have had more than enough suffering in this lifetime. No more of that please, Father.

CHAPTER 12

Seeing My Granddaughter before She Was Born

The Place of Infants Waiting to Be Born

Like all things in this world, you will learn a lot just by looking around with the eyes to see, the ears to hear, and an open mind. This is also true for observing newly born infants through toddlers and small children to about age six. We need to remember that small children, from a time perspective, are closer to God than we are. They have recently been in the spiritual world with direct, unhindered access to God, His angels, and all the other realms of existence. Their memories and feelings do not instantly disappear when they are born. Their memories of the heavenly realm linger for a few years in their young lives here on earth.

I know most people do not really meditate on where the infants come from other than being miracles of God. Some people do believe in reincarnation; others, like a very nice Jesuit priest I knew, do not. I asked him where I was a hundred years ago in a pastoral ministry class. In a big, booming voice, he bellowed these words, "You did not exist." Now this priest really did not *know* from any experience he had. He was just talking Catholic doctrine. But the questions remain. Just when did we take on our spiritual existence, which, Christian doctrine states, is separate from our physical bodies? If we do have separate spiritual bodies as Christian doctrine states, to me, it is necessary to believe our spiritual bodies existed before our physical bodies. Biblical verses talk about us being made in the image of God. This almost completes the argument that the real us, the spiritual us, lived in the spiritual world before we were born as infants. You do not have to believe in Hindu-like reincarnation to believe that our spiritual bodies preexisted our physical bodies. This is true even if you believe we live only once.

After birth, our memories of the spiritual world gradually diminish for a variety of reasons. The reason I connect preexistence, infants, toddlers, and small children is that we can learn about God and the spirit world by really listening to our little ones and watch how they behave without resigning all that to just the way kids are. To varying degrees, children are still under the influence of their recent spiritual existence before birth, and that shows sometimes in what they say and what they do. Toddlers and small children still retain memories of the spiritual world and the beings who inhabit that realm. There are lots of research on this topic that is available online. For me, after doing my due diligence and research on this topic, there is no doubt that our spiritual essence preexists our physical bodies. The following personal experience is proof.

If you have read any of my other books, you will know I write from my own experiences. So too is it with this point about preexistence and some of the nature of that. The following will bring new light to this subject.

A Mystical Event

My daughter-in-law was about seven months pregnant with my first grandchild. I was both nervous and excited about the prospect of becoming a grandfather. Gee, was I already getting that old? Where did the time go? Everyone was so happy about the coming birth and praying that the baby would be healthy. I wanted very much to hold the little one in my arms.

I was tired one evening and went to bed a little early. It had been a normal day and evening—nothing special. I fell asleep like everyone does each evening. But this nightly sleep would turn out to be something far different than normal with an event that was completely unexpected and beyond my control. It remains crystal clear in my memory. I remember every detail like it was just last night. This mystical event is unlike dreams that that we either do not remember when we wake up or are forgotten quickly afterward.

This is one hallmark of a real spiritual event and is not anything related to dreaming.

Without warning, I woke up. But this time it was fantastically different. As I woke up, I realized that my body was still sleeping. Somehow, this felt completely normal but unusual at the same time. I began to slowly travel out the top of my head. As I departed, I could see myself sleeping in bed as if I were on the other side of the wall, seeing through it. I was slowly traveling away from my physical body to a place that I did not know. After a few seconds, I arrived at a place of wonderment and beauty, both in its peace of mind and its appearance. It was like nothing I have ever seen or imagined. Words fail to describe the beauty, peace, and love that existed there.

This place was simple in appearance yet exquisite in its beauty. I cannot put into words how it looked except to say it was as if I arrived in a place that was very soft in nature, a nurturing place that was colored in a light powder blue with lighter tones higher up. I could see no floor, but the spirits there were behaving in their movements as if there was one. It has a certain library kind of feel to it. There were no loud sounds, but rather, there was a peaceful air about being there. I could see multiple little spirits moving about in different directions. They all were moving slowly as if each had a purpose in what they were doing.

Then I understood that what I was watching was a preparation room of some kind for spirit beings who were soon to be born. They all were preparing to live a life here on earth. This became a point of knowledge for me a very short time after I arrived in this realm. Without words, this knowledge was given to me telepathically. I never knew who it was who taught me that for I never saw any other kind of spirit there. The spirit beings I saw were round. Their eyes were very small and dark. Their heads and shoulders were also very rounded in nature. I saw no legs or feet, but they moved about without any effort that I could see. They had a slight blue/white color to them but were also transparent. Those on the other side of the room paid no attention to my presence.

Then I saw that one spirit saw me and approached me. We were face-to-face in this realm of peace. The spirit was lightly transparent and white like all the rest of the spirit beings there. I could see through this spirit as I could all the rest of the spirits. It had small coal-dark eyes. There were no distinct facial features either.

I knew who this spirit was. It was my grandchild, yet to be born. We looked at each other with a deep curiosity without really saying anything to each other. I also knew that my yet-to-be-born grandchild knew who I was. There was a level of shared knowing. After what seemed like a fairly long time of just looking at each other, I said to myself, "This is getting awkward." We just were staring at each other. I guess my little spirit being was wondering what I was doing there. With that thought, I was instantly back in my body, awaking in a normal manner. I woke up on my left side, which is exactly how I saw myself when I traveled outside my body. Needless to say, I was completely amazed about what had just happened. I had the distinct feeling that the realm to which I had I traveled was only a few feet above my head and on the other side of the wall from where I slept.

During the time I was outside my body, I had only feelings of peace and wonderment. I never had any feelings of fright, anxiety, or fear. There were only positive thoughts and feelings the whole time I was outside my body in this other realm, where I saw all those spirits to be born soon.

The implications of this very personal mystical experience are significant regarding a number of theological areas. First, this mystical exposes the truth behind Christian dogma that we are indeed made of mind, body, and spirit. If this were not true, then I would have never been able to see my granddaughter in the spirit and without her physical body in that wonderful place in the spirit world I described. Her body was still forming in her mother's womb. She had not been incarnated yet.

Things do carry over from the spirit world to the physical world. In the case of my granddaughter, when she was very young, she showed a definite preference for me to hold her, and when she started to walk, she would walk up to me and hug my legs, wanting me to carry her far more than others in the room. My interpretation of this is that she remembered me from our visit before she was born. In a world that is so unfamiliar to a little child, you go to what is familiar.

Another implication is obvious. The spirit world actually does exist beyond any doubt. All that I experienced would never have been possible otherwise. If the spirit world exists and the spirit of one child can be seen before birth, then it is not a stretch to believe that our spirits live on after physical death and return to the spirit world. Christian teachings again have pointed to an eternal truth that is very safe to believe in.

Since the spirit world does exist, then that also means that there are higher powers in this creation that we cannot see. They can see us though. And no, that is not scary. These higher powers, also known as God, reign over all creation including the spirit world, and we better live our lives according to what rules have been handed down throughout the ages from the mystics, shamans, priests, rabbis, monks, saints, and other religious authorities.

There is an inexorably strong and permanent connection between the spirit world and the physical world we live in. There are so many ways in which these two realms are manifested for us to observe and experience. There is prayer, the answering of prayer, mystical experiences like the one I described above, feelings that seem to come from nowhere that turn out to greatly benefit the person receiving that, a knowing of something that is not possible through the five senses or something that is going to happen, a warning of something, and last but not least, all the near-death experiences that have been documented over the last twenty years. All this shows beyond any doubt that the spirit world exists, it is there to help us, and it is where we came from and where we are going back to after our life on earth is over.

Most of you already believe what I have said above in faith and love for Jesus Christ and His church. So do I. But I have been given great blessings and grace to have directly experienced these things in my life, and I know that God wants to use me as a person that speaks out the truth about his magnificent creation. Through my words in my books, I want to honor God's truth and His love for all of us and give all my readers real-life examples of what the Christian doctrine teaches us. Faith is great, but direct knowledge through experience is better. I am lucky enough to have both.

What Did God Reveal of Himself?

1. Our spiritual existence is real, and it preexists our being born into this physical realm.

2. God allows little children to remember the spiritual world for a time until the clatter and banging of this physical world drown out the peaceful wonderments of the spiritual realm from which we all have come from.

3. Listen to small children, and let them describe their imaginary friends. Never discourage them from telling you about their experiences before they were born.

4. There is an inexorable connection between this physical realm and the spiritual world. There must be. Otherwise, the

mystical experiences I have had and others have had would not be possible. God wants us to be exposed to the spiritual realm, even while we are in this physical world.

5. There are powerful divine spiritual beings ready to help us according to the will of God. This must be true; otherwise, I would have not been pulled out of my body while I was sleeping and taken to the peaceful place where little spirit beings were preparing to be born into this physical world.

CHAPTER 13

My Ongoing Mystical Life

The Recent Years

One thing I want to emphasize is that exposure to the spiritual realm is available to us each day of our lives. The mystical is always there for us no matter where we are, the time of day, or what we are doing. God is always present and so are other spiritual beings.

For example, in the years since my wife passed away, our communications have taken on a regular and normal tone to them. Gone are the intense feelings that came from recovering from her death and the trauma that accompanied that. We now can indeed communicate for very brief periods of time (a few seconds) with very few words. It seems that most times, she tends to know what is on my mind and will answer yes or no or some other very short sentence even before I get all the words out of my mouth to ask a question. It's not really my mouth for everything is silent with telepathy. This is amazing to me that she knows how I am and what I may be doing. But I do not believe she can see me like other humans do.

In the last few years, her appearance has slowly changed. After she first passed through the veil into heaven, she had a solid appearance.

She would always be behind my right shoulder. I could see her without turning my head. All I had to do was shift my attention to where she was, and I could see her. Over time she gradually became more gossamer looking. It was as if I could plainly see her, but she became more transparent. She always appeared in blue and white that became more flowing with gentle curves. She was becoming increasingly beautiful. She was beautiful to start with, but now her spiritual beauty is increasing.

However, I am not sure if it is me or God not allowing as much communication as before, but it seems that my perceptions of her presence are getting more far apart. I take this to be normal as with all things. This does not bother me, though. It is because I have found a wonderful woman who loves me as I love her. It is a strange experience to lose someone you love so much and for so long in death and then years later have a loving relationship with someone else. I believe that God has provided for me, and I know Marilyn had something to do with this too. I know she approves since my special one makes me happy. It is a very strange feeling for me, to love and miss my wife while at the same time being able to love another wonderful woman. I guess it is like loving all three of my children at the same time.

I continue to rest in the arms of my Father and know that I will see all the people I love who have already gone to heaven like my Grandpa and Grandma Troha and my aunts and uncles. But don't let that last sentence fool you. Living this life continues to be a challenge. But with the love of my special sweetheart, I know the rest of my life will be good.

Jesus and Our Virgin Mary Consoled Me

I am writing this part of the book immediately after a meditation session where some very remarkable events occurred. These kinds of things do not always happen. But in my life, it seems that God has smiled upon me for reasons I do not know. What most people regard as highly unusual spiritual events are more of a regular part of my life.

This does not make me better in any way than anyone else. This gift of spiritual or mystical events brings with it a higher degree of suffering in my life and more divine responsibility.

It is a serious responsibility that I represent mystical events exactly as they occur without any embellishments or exaggeration. I also believe that my physical sufferings are directly related to the mystical events I experience. I have come to believe that my ailments are God's way of slowing me down, so I spend time alone in meditation, and this allows the door of my heart to be open to connecting with God in a much deeper way. You see, I suffer from clinical depression, and it is a constant, daily battle for me. There are many times in my life where my only refuge is meditation and praying to our Father in heaven.

However, on this particular occasion, after I played golf one day, I was very tired. The previous day, I had a migraine that ruined my plans to do things with my beautiful girlfriend. I was praying to our Blessed Virgin Mary and to our Lord Jesus Christ. I prayed to the Blessed Virgin to please give me consolation for my continual heartache and feelings of depression that occurred for no good reason and whenever they wanted to. I had everything to be thankful for and yet feelings of dread, anxiety, and fearfulness many times over take me because of the way that my nervous system has been wired since birth.

As I was on the couch with my eyes closed, the Blessed Virgin Mary came to me off my right side. I did not expect this at all. I could see her even though my eyes were closed. This was indeed a vision of the Blessed Virgin Mary. She was dressed in blue and white robes, which is common to the depiction of her within the Catholic Church. However, I could not see her face. I do not know why. I said to her, "My dearest mother in heaven. I ask for your consolation and to feel your loving warmth and your touch to help me deal with these feelings that I have that are born out of my traumatic existence and the biology of my physical body."

In a very loving voice, all she said was, "My dear son." But the way in which she said it was so loving, so sincere, so all-encompassing, and with the deepest affection that it helped me tremendously. There was tremendous empathy in her voice and the energy that flowed around her. She was magnificent in every way I can think of. It was as if she knew me far better than anyone else who knows me. But that was not all which was to come during this very special meditation.

After a short time, while our Blessed Virgin Mary was still present in the room with me, our Lord Jesus Christ also appeared. I could see Jesus Christ with much more clarity than I could our Blessed Virgin. I saw him in a way that I have never seen before. He appeared like no other image of him that I have ever seen. No statue, no painting, or no other image of Jesus was anything like what I saw during my meditation and the vision that I saw of our Lord and Savior Jesus Christ. His face was more rounded than any image I have ever seen. His cheeks looked full. He did have a full beard that was cropped relatively short. His hair was curly and very dark. It was not long like many depictions of Jesus that we all have seen. The color of his hair was either very dark brown or black. He did have bushy eyebrows. His nose was not thin, but rather a little wide, and he had dark-colored eyes. His skin tone was also a little on the dark side. In most images we see of Jesus, he is relatively tall. However, when I saw him, he was relatively short. All of this was surprising to me.

Regarding his clothes, his outer garment was a white robe, and his inner garment was red. I could not see his feet or those of our Blessed Virgin Mary.

I asked Jesus, "Please, dear Lord, take away the suffering I have with my headaches, my asthma, my allergies, and my clinical depression." Jesus responded by saying, "Not yet, my dear son, not yet." To me, this was both good news and bad news. The manner in which he responded told me that my infirmities would not be taken away, but perhaps sometime in the future they would.

So I shall wait patiently for God's healing. I have complete faith that God will do exactly what Jesus said he would do. All this happened in a very quiet and darkened room, and I was in deep meditative thought with my heart, my spiritual heart, outstretched toward both our Blessed Virgin Mary and Jesus Christ. And both of them responded to me in a very loving manner. What a wonderful experience to have knowing that both the Blessed Virgin Mary and Jesus Christ took a complete interest in what is happening in my life, my problems, and my infirmities, and they responded to me as I was praying.

I also know that anyone who prays will also have their prayers answered in many different ways. Seeing our Blessed Virgin Mary and our Lord Jesus Christ is one way in which prayers are answered. However, there are many others. One must completely open their hearts to God and devote their lives and their very existence to God in heaven. Then these things may happen in your life, as well. I am not special. God and our Blessed Virgin Mary and Jesus Christ are certainly available to all those who seek our Father in heaven and pray earnestly from their heart.

Medical Quackery

There was a time about ten years ago where I made a trip to our orchard in Bakersfield California. I managed the family ranch there for a number of years. I had purchased a new handgun and was anxious to see how it performed. I took it out into the middle of the orchard, loaded it up, and aimed at the base of a tree. I shot three times in succession and hit the tree. All three times I was happy with the performance of the handgun. However, instantly after I shot three bullets, my ears began to ring very loudly. Yours truly forgot to put hearing protection on. This was really stupid, but nonetheless, that is what I forgot to do.

The ringing in my ears was intense and continued for a couple of weeks. I then decided to go to an ear specialist to find out what I could do about reducing the amount of ringing. The doctor I went to put me through some tests that I thought didn't make any sense, like putting me into a darkened, quiet room, and I heard beeping sounds in my ears with electrodes attached to my skull. All I wanted to find out was what I could do to stop the ringing. But there I was, getting a test I didn't think I needed. The test came out just fine, and then as an afterthought, the doctor said, "Oh, while you are here, let me feel your thyroid gland." She told me I had a lump on my thyroid gland and immediately the doctor started talking about the percentage rates of cancer. Needless to say, this greatly upset me because I was in my mid-forties when this happened.

So, I was told I had to schedule for a biopsy with the receptionist. While talking to her, she happened to mention that the doctor removed her thyroid, too. Red flags started to fly. What are the chances of having two thyroids removed? I was very upset at the prospect of surgery and losing my thyroid, which means medication for the rest of my life. I went to my car and started to drive out of the parking lot when a very strong voice told me telepathically, "It is nothing." There was no mistaking this intervention of the spirit world to reassure me to ignore what the doctor told me. I instantly felt a strong sense of relief and peace that came over me. From that moment on, I was relieved and felt that I was just being scammed by a doctor. I never really worried about my thyroid. Again.

A couple of months later I went to see my regular physician, and while I was there, I asked him if he would examine my thyroid. He examined it for at least three or four minutes, and he said, "Rich, I just cannot feel anything unusual there." He went on to say that he is very good at detecting thyroid abnormalities, but he found nothing, and my thyroid was normal. Then I told him the story of the specialist I went to. He shook his head and didn't know what else to say other than the fact that I was normal. The spiritual being that told me it was nothing was indeed correct. Again.

To further confirm the truthfulness of divine spirituality, another month later, I went to visit my allergy doctor. While I was there, I also asked him to inspect my thyroid. This doctor also could find nothing wrong and asked me why I was concerned about my thyroid. Then I told him the story. He told me, "Rich, the ringing in your ears will slowly go away. I would not worry about it." And my doctor was right. Over the next month, the ringing slowly went.

It was the mystical intervention of a spirit being very close to me that told me as I was leaving the first doctor's parking lot not to worry about it that allowed me to keep my sanity, for I had a lot of burdens on the raising of three children, providing for them, and their financial security.

Prostate Cancer

As I write this, I am in the midst of dealing with prostate cancer. Last week, a specialist examined me and diagnosed me with prostate cancer. When the doctor told me it was 100% that I had prostate cancer I really did not get upset. Somehow I had a feeling of peace within myself. Somehow the spirit world informed me that everything would be OK. However, to us stuck in this physical world, it still means needing medical treatment, which will be successful in eradicating what I currently have. In the week since I was diagnosed, I have been giving myself Reiki treatments and praying to God to let this really be nothing in the long term of my life. I know I have much more to do here. And if I am to do it according to God's will, my prostate cancer will be completely healed. Yet I will still need some surgery and radiation. Well...Ok if that is what is needed so I can continue on doing what I am here for.

I have to say that since I do know the spiritual world and have been there multiple times and have had many mystical experiences beyond the ones that I have documented in this book, I am really getting tired of putting up with all the problems within this physical world that we all live in. But I have a specific mission to accomplish. Just like each of you do. I am determined to finish my assignments so that I will never have to come back again to complete them. My real home is that in the spiritual realm just as yours is.

Because of what the divine spirit being told me—that "it is nothing"—I have complete confidence that whatever treatment I receive will be successful. And then I will pick up the pieces of my life and continue on. At this point, it is ever so clear to me that I am living my life for the benefit of others and not for me. And this really is one of the essential essences of Christianity. We live our lives to benefit God's children. We are not here to grab what we can while we can for our own purposes but rather be of service to other of God's children to meet their needs and increase the quality of their lives as much as we can.

I believe this is why the spirit being told me that my prostate cancer was "nothing." It was so I can continue to write this book and not worry about what is going to happen next medically for me. Remember, God is closer to you than your own breath. He knows the number of hairs on your head. He knows you better than you know yourself. He knows what is bothering you, what you are thinking, and what actions you may take next. This is why He sends messengers to us. If we have our minds open and our hearts attuned to God, we will hear His messengers just as I heard the message about my prostate cancer and all manner of other things during the course of my life.

One last thought, after all the treatments my radiation oncologist told me that it looks like this cancer thing will just be "a bump in the road" for me. This occurred a few months after my mystical encounter telling me not to worry about it.

CHAPTER 14

The Dark Side

Satanic Evil Comes at Me as I Sleep

Most people associate mystical events with those of the sacred and divine. This is certainly true, and the vast majority of all my mystical experiences have come from God and the heavenly realm. But we must remember that Jesus Christ Himself encountered demons and Satan himself during His three years of ministry. This is conclusive proof that the dark side does exist. Make no mistake. Hell is very real and waiting for those who do not accept Jesus Christ and live according to His teachings to the best of their abilities.

There were two times in my life where I personally encountered the horrid blackness of the dark side. The first time, I encountered a powerful demon or possibly Satan himself. I am not sure which. The event occurred in my early to midthirties. It was during this time in my life that the real Christianity of my inner being was awakening. I had attended a number of Billy Graham revivals in San Jose, California, and was reading the Bible daily. I also many times got up early before work and jogged five miles while listening to a Bible broadcast on the radio while running.

I got to thinking that wouldn't life be wonderful if there were no evil in the world—that there was no suffering, no killing, and no cruelty? Knowing that the devil, or Satan, is the author of all untruths and is actively working against the will of God, I got angry at the devil. Sporadically, I would curse the devil for all the suffering and meanness in the world. I directed my comments directly at him. This went on for a number of weeks.

Somehow, this made me feel like I was more of a courageous Christian. But truth be told, I was still a neophyte Christian, not yet solidly grounded as I thought I was.

After being angry with Satan for a while, one night, I went to sleep. My wife slept next to me. Sometime during the wee hours of the morning, a very large black cloud came directly at me. I was sleeping, but this inky black cloud came right at me while I slept. I cannot explain how I was sleeping, but I saw all this terrifying sight. Then an extremely loud and booming voice yelled these words directly at me, "I will get you!" This torrential black cloud completely enveloped me. It was filled with hate and anger beyond description and was threatening to take me with it into what I knew was hell. I knew this horrifying threat was hell's direct response to my cursing the devil.

It was the most frightening and scary voice I had ever heard in my entire life. It suddenly woke me up, and I gasped for breath. My heart was pounding. I could feel beads of sweat forming on my forehead. I instantly thought this booming voice must have awoken everybody in the house. I literally could feel his voice trying to tear at my very existence with a demonic hatred that was utterly complete with its horrific desire to consume me and take me down into the bastions of hell. I sat up in bed, I looked over to my right, and there was my wife peacefully sleeping. Our older kids were also sleeping peacefully in their bedrooms.

I was the only one who heard the crashing ugliness and hateful gnashing tone of this evil voice directed right at me. I was so scared I was shaking. As I gathered my senses over the next few minutes, I realized that everything and everyone in the house was safe and sound and peacefully sleeping. I was very tempted to wake my wife and ask, "Did you hear that?" But I didn't. I did not want to scare her because of what had just happened. I lay there for a while, trying to convince myself that it was just a bad dream. But it wasn't. It was so very real. And I knew who it was. It most definitely was Satan threatening me because of what I had cursed at him. After I calmed down, I told myself that I would never do that again. At the same time, though, I was not the slightest bit deterred from my Christian faith.

It took me quite a while to get over this horribly frightening experience. I have never cursed at the devil again. Never before in my life have I had an experience so intense, murderous, hateful, surprising, and instantly overwhelming beyond anything I can really describe. Over the next several years, I slowly began to realize that the devil really has no power over us. Really, all we have to do is not pay attention to demonic threats, for in doing so, we give the evil side the energy that it can use against us. Just do not give them any energy. Also, I realized that God has given us dominion over evil forces in our lives. We just have to make sure through our own free will that we choose good over any evil temptations or threats that may come our way. This would prove to be true in my second direct encounter with evil forces.

Evil Hate Comes at Me during a Reiki Session

It would be years later that I had the second experience with another black cloud coming directly at me. By this time, I had become a Reiki master and performed many sessions for the benefit of people in need, including nurses at the oncology ward in Good Samaritan Hospital. The cloud came during a Reiki session I was conducting for a client in that person's home. It was here that my second experience with a terrible and frightful evil spirit came at me inside another inky black cloud. But this time, I had no fear at all for I knew without any doubt that God had given me the strength I needed over threats from demons and evil black clouds.

This second time was filled with just as much blackness, utter pure hate seeking complete destruction, and the complete willful desire to destroy me any way it could. But this time, my reaction was completely different. This particular person receiving Reiki healing energy had a mother whom I would classify as a dark spirit. This person was seeking to overcome both the emotional and psychological effects of what was done by the mother when this person was a young child. Normally, there are seventeen different Reiki hand positions used in the normal course of a treatment, which lasts between forty and forty-five minutes. However, during this session, my hands were guided to depart from some of the normal hand positions, and I placed my right hand under my client's neck. I also placed the other hand on my client's forehead.

That is when all hell broke loose. As is the case for Reiki masters such as myself, I always pray to God for guidance, life-giving energy to flow through me into my client, and protection for the both of us. When I placed my right hand under the back of my client's neck, instantly and although my eyes were closed, I saw again a monstrous and hideous inky-black cloud coming directly toward me. In the center of this black cloud was the face of a woman. She had black hair and dark eyes and had a horribly angry expression on her face that was filled with hate and cruelty. It was instantly obvious. Her intent was to destroy me because she knew I was a child of God helping her child to recover from all the destructive things she had done.

This time, however, I was not the slightest bit scared. I simply said these words, "Dear Lord, send your angels to protect us." Instantly, almost before I got those words out of my mind, I felt the presence of at least twenty angels, and I could see images of them surround the bed my client was on. With that, I looked directly at the woman in the black cloud, and I commanded her, "Go away, go back to hell where you came from, by the authority of the Lord Jesus Christ." And only in a matter of a second, the black cloud with a woman in it started to recede and got smaller and smaller and smaller. You must remember that in order to defeat evil, all you must do is make the right choices— ask for God's assistance and guidance.

Know full well that God will never ever fail you, and with the power of His love, evil will be forced to obey you and recede back to where it came from. Now, as it turns out, after this black cloud seemingly disappeared, I saw with my spiritual eyes that there were just the slightest wisps of black cloud still remaining in the upper-right corner of the room. I looked at it, and I said in a stern voice, "I told you to go away! Go!" The final remnants of this evil black cloud then silently and instantly disappeared, never to be seen again. From that point on, I continued with my Reiki session for the benefit of my client.

Yes, the dark side is real. From the direct testimony of other people on their deathbeds or people who have had near-death experiences, the reality of the existence of hell is indeed part of what we must deal with. I remind you again. Accept the love of our Lord Jesus Christ and live as best as you possibly can according to all His sacred teachings. Jesus is indeed the way, the truth, and the life.

A Real Mystical Experience or a Nightmare?

Some people may wonder whether my first story was anything more than a really bad nightmare and not a true mystical experience. My thoughts on this are that it was definitely a nasty mystical experience rooted in the darkness of hell itself. There are a number of reasons for this, which are consistent with the general character of a mystical experience versus a nightmare.

I realize now that my cursing the devil for weeks before this incident happened amounted to taunting the devil. It is completely consistent with an evil being to respond as forcefully as possible. Human nightmares are usually rooted in things that occur within the physical realm and not the spiritual realm as this one did. I have had nightmares before as a child but never as an adult, and this event was a hundred times worse than the worst nightmares I'd had. This carried with it a threat to my existence, which no nightmare of mine ever did previously.

Consistent with communications from the spirit world, it was only I that could hear the bellowing black beast. Not even my wife next to me had any idea of what was happening. I did not toss and turn as is the case with many nightmares. This entire episode took less than a minute. Carried within this nasty mystical experience was a subliminal message. That subliminal message was simply that evil spirits or the devil do not waste time on good Christian people unless they are headed toward a lifetime of significantly furthering God's will on this earth. I am humbled to say that my lifetime activities have resulted in much good being done for many people, and I believe that Satan knew this and wanted to scare me out of what my divine destiny entailed. Again, I have to say this with complete humility with all credit, glory, and honor going to God our Father and our Lord Jesus Christ, for without them, I can do nothing.

The second dark event happened when I had full protection from God and was far more spiritually mature. I was no longer the freshman Christian who could be frightened by evil beings. I realized and knew without a doubt that good always triumphs over evil in the end, and each of us has the power to reject evil as long as we invoke the love of Jesus Christ.

What Did God Reveal of Himself?

1. Evil spiritual entities do exist. Perhaps you have had a similar experience or maybe you know of someone who has. Remember, you are safe in the arms of our eternally loving God.

2. They do not have dominion over our own free will and over our capacity to love. Give them no energy or thought. Just focus on loving as best you know how, and ask God for his divine guidance and protection. You will be just fine. From my own experience, I know this to be true.

3. Evil spirits may scare you like they did when I was in my early thirties, but God has given us power over them, and all we need to do is to not dwell on whatever power we imagine they may have.

4. Again, they do not have power over us. Do not give evil spiritual entities any energy by means of your thoughts about them or being frightened of them. Remember, we are all children of God, and calling upon God our Father or Jesus Christ directly will instantly result in overcoming any evil spirits that may come your way.

5. Always remember what Jesus said: "Fear not!"

CHAPTER 15

What Is It Like to Be a Reiki Master?

Why I Became a Reiki Master

One of the most significant events in my life was becoming spiritually attuned to become a Reiki practitioner. I will never forget the warmth in my heart that I felt after my first attunement. I felt so much closer to God, and I sensed that our Lord was very pleased with what I was doing in pursuing a healing ministry with Reiki.

The reason I chose this sacred healing path was because of my wife's cancer. I would stop at nothing to heal her in any way I could. My spiritual advisor mentioned to me during one session about Reiki that she knew a Reiki master I could go to and become attuned to deliver healing energy to my wife. Needless to say, I jumped at the chance. Within a few weeks, became a level 1 Reiki practitioner. Everything I learned about Reiki, the universal life energy of God that permeates creation, and how that energy flows through a person that is attuned is all consistent with Christianity and the major religions of the world. It all made sense to me, and all that I learned in graduate pastoral ministry school. It is consistent with how the spiritual world constantly interacts with the physical world.

After practicing Reiki with quite a number of people, I got very good at it and proceeded through more attunements. I developed my own style, so to speak, which is very God-centered and spiritual. These additional attunements ultimately allowed me to attain Reiki master status. Becoming a Reiki practitioner and then a Reiki master is something that will always remain with me for my whole life. It forms a permanent channel between me and God. That channel allows God's divine healing energy to flow through me and into my client where it may heal mind, body, and spirit. I am humbled at the thought of this.

If you are like some people and worry that Reiki is some sort of illegitimate spiritual hocus pocus, I understand that concern. But it is misplaced. I am here to tell you as a committed Christian and Reiki master that anything you hear like this is due to ignorance of the true nature of Reiki and God's direct involvement with that kind of healing for his children. I can tell you that as a Reiki master, the healing I am involved with is similar to what Jesus Christ did while He was on this earth. I am by no means Jesus Christ, though, and I do not have the powers of Jesus Christ. Our Lord Jesus is set above all men always for He is the son of God. I am a created being who strives to be as much like Jesus Christ as I can. I feel very blessed by God that I have been led to a ministry of healing using the healing modality of Reiki, for I can testify to you that it has helped a lot of people. This is what my clients tell me. It has also helped me in my Christian spiritual life.

Reiki is an intelligent healing energy that first goes to where it is needed most. This includes mind, body, and soul. Because of this directionality to where it is needed most, it could be that a client may have a sore knee but needs spiritual healing more. Reiki will go to that person's spirit first, and it may appear that Reiki failed for the knee will subsequently show no progress. But this is the way things work for the ultimate benefit of God's children. If you think about it, it makes sense to be this way. In this example, God cares more about a person's spirit than He would a knee.

What Does It Feel Like to Be a Reiki Master?

I remember very clearly how I felt after I attained the first level of Reiki practitioner. Driving home, I felt very much closer to God. Although I have been a Christian my whole life, I somehow felt that God was more real and closer to me than I had ever experienced before. It was as if there were a loving presence around me. Of course, God's loving presence had been there all along, but now for the first time, I experienced it in a deeper way. This perception of a deeper presence of God has never left me to this day. Frankly, it has deepened further over the years.

After about a year of gaining experience by performing Reiki sessions among a lot of different people and for different reasons, I ascended through the levels and became a Reiki master. It was during this time that I increasingly felt a strong sense of humility and realized in a more deeply that I was truly a servant of God for the benefit of His other children.

I became far more effective and creative in the use of the Reiki healing modality and God's healing energy that flows through me. I continue to be amazed at how the human chakras work and how they could be used to diagnose various issues of health and well-being for the people I worked with.

If there is anybody who doubts Reiki or the existence of chakras, just do the following: Hold out your hand with the palm up and the fingers flat. Get a necklace of any kind made of any material, and with the other hand, hold the necklace above the center of the outstretched palm of your other hand. Hold the end of the necklace still about one inch above your flattened palm on the other hand. In a few moments, you will see the necklace start to rotate counterclockwise as if some invisible force was working on it.

This invisible force is a minor chakra of everyone's body. This is real human spiritual energy manifesting itself in a physical way that you can see with your own eyes. Now flip your flattened hand over so the palm is facing down. Hold the necklace over the back of your hand, and you will see it now rotate clockwise. It is opposite of the way it rotated with the palm up. It is these energies that mainstream scientists have totally ignored or shoved to the side. It is these kinds of energies that Reiki masters work with to increase the health of a person's mind, body, and spirit. This is no trick of some kind, but a real manifestation of spiritual energies of the human body that everyone has, and it can be seen by anyone who does the above little experiment.

I also want to emphasize that because Reiki masters work with God's healing energy, it is totally impossible to do any harm to a person during a Reiki session. This is unlike regular physicians who may prescribe the wrong treatments for a patient and end up doing more harm than good. The worst thing that can happen with a Reiki session is nothing. There is never a negative result because again it is God's loving and healing energy we are working with.

I have had many different experiences with people in the years I have been a Reiki master. I have even experienced chakras running backward, indicating a very serious emotional condition with one person I worked with. After the Reiki session with this person, I had it healed and running forward again, which is a direct indication of the power of God's healing energy that runs through Reiki practitioners and masters for the benefit of the people they work with.

On another occasion, for example, a man asked me to heal his knee. I went to his house and performed a complete Reiki session concentrating on his sore knee that prevented him from walking up and down the stairs due to a lot of pain. After the first session, he told me he felt much better and exclaimed that he felt like he could run up the stairs. This was great. But during the session, I also found out that he had incipient heart problems. I asked him if he ever had any issues with his heart. He said that his younger brother passed away two years earlier due to a heart attack. This confirmed to me what I was seeing and feeling about his physical condition.

I suggested to him that he should consider going to a cardiac doctor just to confirm he was okay. I saw this gentleman one more time for his knee, and I asked if he saw a cardiac doctor yet. Without him answering, I knew he had not. The result of my two sessions with this man was that his knee was indeed much better, but he would not ever see a doctor at my suggestion. That is, until he really needed one. He never asked me back since he knew I would ask him again about the cardiac examination. Sometimes being a Reiki master leads you to find things your client wishes to ignore, like this gentleman.

In my life, being a Reiki master has bridged the gap between the spirit world and the physical world. I have seen directly the effects of spiritual energy and how it operates within the physical world. In that sense, I feel extremely blessed and humbled to have become a Reiki master and to help God's other children become healthier in mind, body, and spirit. I have begun to see that there is a continuum of existence between the physical world and the unseen spiritual world. Both these worlds or realms are tightly intertwined in a way that almost everybody in this world is not aware of. Becoming a Reiki master has allowed me to perceive the nature of how the physical world and the spiritual world are intertwined and constantly interacting. It is a wonderful and constant experience to live life and realize this every day that I wake up. Being a Reiki master has also led to other spiritual gifts that have allowed me to perceive more clearly the nature of the spiritual world that awaits us after we passed from this physical world. I will not go to any details of this now, for it is documented in other parts of this book.

So in summary, what is it like to be a Reiki master? It has made me feel empowered from a spiritual perspective. Yet at the same time I feel very humbled that God would have chosen me and allowed me this blessing. It has increased my knowledge of God immensely. And as a result, when I speak of God, it comes from my direct experience of Him and His love for all His children and for all creation. Being a Reiki master has allowed me to write this book with spiritual authority, for everything that I say has come from my direct experience and not from any reference material or anything else that may have been written in the spiritual literature. This is why you will find no reference material or footnotes or quotes in this book. It is all originated from my personal experiences.

What It Feels Like to Perform a Reiki Session

Conducting a Reiki session is a very prayerful and powerful experience. I always start each Reiki session with a prayer to God our Father and God our Mother. I ask that God's healing energy flow through me and into my client's body where it may go to heal in mind, body, and spirit. The beginning prayer takes about two minutes, and this sets the tone for the rest of the forty- or forty-five-minute session. There are seventeen different hand positions that are standard in performing a Reiki session. However, I let God guide my hands to nonstandard positions as well, depending upon how I feel I am being guided by God. I do not pray to Reiki guides, for they have no ability to heal. Only God does. Like my good friend and Jesuit brother always says, we can do nothing except by the power of God. This certainly applies to Reiki healing, as well.

As a Reiki session progresses, images will come to me as far as what the true nature of the ailment may be. Also, I can get feelings of what may be bothering my client, either spiritually or emotionally, in addition to anything physical that may be going on. I use the main chakras and their strength to help locate additional difficulties that my client may be experiencing. While I am giving a Reiki session, I feel ever so close to God. I can feel God's healing energy flowing through me.

There are also strong physical manifestations that I feel during some Reiki sessions. Many times, I will experience very intense waves of tingling that start at the top of my head and slowly work their way downward through my entire body and into my feet. I have to tell you that this is the most pleasurable feeling that the human being could possibly experience. When these occurrences of intense and magnificently pleasurable tingling are happening to me during a Reiki session, I wish so very much that they would never end. It is that pleasurable. These occurrences of intense and pleasurable tingling usually last about two or three minutes. There are usually three waves of intense pleasure. Then, regrettably, they fade away. Also, when this happens, I know that a tremendous amount of healing energy is flowing through me to my client, which gives me a very deep sense of fulfillment and satisfaction because the connection between God and me and the client is very strong.

Other physical sensations I experience during Reiki sessions include my hands getting very warm to the point where my client says they feel hot. For those of you who are scientifically inclined, I can tell you that this heat is not a result of the radiant infrared energy coming from my client's body. Rather, it comes from the energy that is flowing through me into the client. People receiving Reiki also have told me on numerous occasions that even though my hands are lightly touching the top of their head, their feet may start to tingle. This is a normal occurrence when it happens. But to clients, it seems really weird.

During a Reiki session, I always repeat my private mantra to God, much like you would during a session of meditation. It's a very simple mantra that I will either say to myself, or if the client wishes, I will softly pray it out loud.

In a nutshell, during a Reiki session, images will appear in my mind from the inner being of my client. My hands warm up. I sometimes get the wonderfully intense tingling sensations that I wish would never go away. I have to say that performing a Reiki session is a spiritual high for me as a Reiki master. Knowing that I'm doing good for my client is something that is wonderful in and of itself. I hope this very short description of what it's like for a Reiki master to perform a session gives you a good idea of what Reiki is all about and what it feels like for a master to perform the sessions. It is all good because it is of God.

Performing a Reiki session is indeed very mystical for it involves God, the Reiki master, another person or client and a deep connection between the divine and sacred spiritual world. That connection between realms manifests itself in different ways with many times resulting is strong physical sensations. There is no other reasonable explanation of these physical sensations other than the deep and abiding connection between God's heavenly realm and the physical realm we live in.

What Did God Reveal of Himself?

1. Being a Reiki master has the divine spiritual power to change your life by bringing God closer to you in unmistakable ways.

2. Being the intersection between this physical realm and the spiritual realm puts the Reiki master in a position to experience real divine spiritual power and removes any lingering doubts about the next world, its existence, and the truth of the Bible.

3. The divine spirit world does exist, and it has power to know what goes on in this physical world. There is an inexorable connection between the divine and this world that God has designed in creation that allows his healing power to have a direct effect on a person's mind, body, and spirit.

4. You can take the healing power manifested by a Reiki master as proof of God's existence and His love for all his children.

5. Reiki is completely consistent with Christian values. Those who say differently do not understand as much as they should.

Those who embrace Reiki's healing, in my view, have an open spirituality. Those who reject are more closed. Open spirituality is a healthy relationship with God, for God is infinite and we are always learning something new of God's character and creation—if we have an open mind and spirit to do so. A more closed spirituality imposes human limitations on God's power and, by its nature, is not healthy and stifles spiritual growth to the potential God intended from the beginning of creation.

Conclusion

What Should We Conclude from All These Mystical Events?

We have traveled a lot of spiritual distance in this book. There are so many things to understand about God and creation from all the events, meditations, and experiences I have had. I remain convinced that God has put me on this earth to not only experience these events but also to communicate them to those special people who have the open mind, heart, and soul to accept as true what is contained in this book. I know that if you are reading this, you too are one of the people I have been put here on earth to tell my life's spiritual story to you.

To really understand the mystical experiences I have had, we need to first understand the basic fabric of God's creation. If we look only at science, we are automatically limiting ourselves to only the physical material realm, the realm our five senses limit us to. That is a tragedy, but it is only way the vast majority of people understand creation. This makes sense since it is only the physical realm that our five senses respond to. That is unless you listen to your inner being and become aware that the physical is only a minor portion of the magnificent creation God has brought forth, which includes the infinite unseen realms that we refer to as the spiritual realm.

Science has made terrific progress in understanding so many things within the physical realm. But unfortunately, science can say nothing about the spirit world. The reason for this is simple. If you cannot measure it, science can say nothing about it. Something that is immeasurable, according to science, does not exist. Yet love itself is immeasurable, and no one will dispute its existence. If you cannot write an equation about it, science remains mute and can say nothing. But there are some scientists, smart as they are, who remain tempted to venture into the theological world.

This is not to demean science in any way. Science has brought us tremendous progress within the physical realm and has made life easier for us in innumerable ways. I myself also have a scientific background with a bachelor's degree in chemistry and have worked at NASA in its planetary branch doing research. But science is limited and will never find God through equations, theoretical studies, or theories about physical things. God does not reside in the physical, although part of creation does.

One of the biggest questions within science today is what happened at the Big Bang, the very start of the universe that we call home. Science can say nothing about what happened before the big bang. All equations completely self-destruct into a series of infinities. This simply means that scientists just don't know. Stephen Hawking, famed theoretical physicist, wrote a book about his equations regarding the beginning of the universe. In his book, he states that something can indeed come from nothing. Quantum physics does allow this to be a possibility. He therefore concludes that we "do not need a God in order to explain the beginning of the universe." I find this to be a particularly sad conclusion on his part.

Again, he cannot explain through equations, no matter how elegant they may seem, what the driving force really was in bringing creation into existence. I believe that Stephen Hawking is overindulging himself in the fantasy that equations of the physical world have a legitimacy being able to explain those things that lie directly within the realm of theology. He has certainly overstepped his bounds and has made a theological fool of himself in the process. I do cut him lots of slack in his wrong assertions as he has not had the benefit of the mystical experiences I have been gifted with. Why God has chosen me, I do not know.

On the other hand, theology cannot tell us the nature of the physical realm like science can, but it can tell us about the *why* the universe exists. The limitations of theology include the fact that if one just studies only theology, we would never be able to invent, for example, the internal combustion engine, the transistor, the laser, the rockets that have taken us to the moon, and many of the wondrous inventions like the Internet and the cell phone, which we all take for granted in our society today. This is not to say, however, that theology plays a secondary role to science. In fact, it is my strong feeling that it is quite the opposite. It is theology that gives us the moral law of the universe. It gives us the reason for our existence. Theology gives us the reason why we are here and what happens after our personal death. It also tells us something about our existence before we came to this physical realm we call earth—in other words, our spiritual preexistence.

Theology gives us the godly moral guidance that steers our increasing command of the physical realm that will benefit mankind. Without godly guidance, both on an individual scale and the scale of all mankind, we will end up destroying ourselves.

If you wish to have a complete understanding of creation, you must understand both the physical scientific realm and the spiritual realm together. It is my strong belief that they are inexorably intertwined in such a way that one needs the other. To understand all the beautiful creation that God has brought into existence, both an intimate relationship with God and a scientific understanding is necessary. So what is the true essence of creation? God says we are eternal beings. This means the spiritual. All things physical cannot last for eternity. It has something to do with what scientists call entropy. I will not explain that here, but it has to do with the amount of chaos in a closed system.

I believe that the true underlying essence of all eternal creation is really a divine matrix of love that connects kindred spirits together in eternal bliss that helps each individual propel themselves to higher and higher realms of spiritual existence in understanding and always coming closer and closer to God himself, whatever you conceive him to be. It allows each spiritual being, you and me, to grow spiritually closer and closer to our infinite and unconditionally loving God. Part of our spiritual growth requires that we spend some time in this physical realm to learn and experience things that we cannot do elsewhere.

This is why the spiritual realm and the physical realm are connected so tightly. It allows God to bring forth mystical experience to those of us who are in the physical world. These mystical experiences allow us to overcome hardship and suffering and bring meaning, eternal meaning, to what it is we are suffering at the time and gives us the strength to endure and succeed in pulling through whatever hardships we may face and ultimately therefore grow closer to God and his infinite wisdom that He wishes to give all His children.

Some of what I just said can be interpreted to depart from Christian doctrine, which says we never existed before we were born and we have only one lifetime on this earth. Then we are judged to determine if we should go to hell or heaven. To me, this does not sound like an unconditionally loving God, which is another doctrine of the Catholic religion. The two thoughts seem diametrically opposed to each other. It is my strong belief that we cannot accomplish everything we need to in spiritual growth for us during just one physical lifetime. If you doubt this, just look at the very poor people of the world where their entire life is consumed only by searching for their next meal. This does not allow them to grow spiritually closer to God in the more complete way we can in developed countries.

Their spiritual growth is stunted by the physical situation they find themselves in. A loving God would give these poor people other chances to grow closer to him, and this means more than one life and chances to learn, experience new things, and grow closer to God through the experiences available in this physical realm. Therefore, I believe that God gives us as many chances as we need to grow as close to Him as we can. But this idea does not sit well with many people. It is understandable. After class one evening in a graduate pastoral ministry class, I asked the priest teaching the class where we all were a hundred years ago. The question was obviously about preexistence. The priest at Santa Clara University told me I did not exist before I was born. The way he said that indicated that he thought that was a stupid question.

Well, it wasn't. I believe that priest was completely wrong. Actually, I say this from my own personal mystical experience. Other mystical experiences I have not discussed in this book point strongly in the direction of what many people would call reincarnation. But this kind of reincarnation is not like the Hindu religion where we are caught in an endless cycle of life and death and life and death until we find nirvana. It is not like that at all.

When we intelligently combine what we know of open-minded theology and open-minded theoretical physics and other disciplines of science, we can only really describe the two realms of existence as one continuous realm of the spiritual and the physical, each continuously affecting the other. It is the spiritual realm and the physical realm that some of us are able to perceive. These two realms are tightly interwoven where events in one affect what happens in the other.

The spiritual is where our true home is and where divine beings exist doing God's will and extending his love and will for us into the physical where we temporarily exist. The godly spiritual divine beings know all there is to know about those of us who dwell in the physical world. They know about our aspirations, our thoughts, our emotions, and the events that happened to us. They deeply love us and are keenly aware of all the other aspects of our current existence. They understand what we are trying to accomplish in the time we have on earth. We are well-known to those divine spiritual beings whose exquisite love for us here in the physical is an integral part of God's creation. Always remember that it is this divine love that transcends the veil and showers us with protection from all that which is not God's will for us. But it does remain our responsibility to use our free will to abide by the divine guidance available to us. We will still have trials and tribulations in our lives, for it is the way we grow in spirit by how we respond to our troubles.

It is God whom we can turn to for help during times of stress and suffering and fretting over what to do next so that we may bring to fruition that which is God's will for us and those around us. One of the ways God himself helps us do this is through mystical experiences for us so that we may stay on the path that God wants us to. In my case, there have been uncountable times I have spoken to my deceased wife. God has allowed this. She has helped me avoid tragic. The story about Megan is one very good example. If I stayed with her, it would have been a first-class tragedy for my entire family. More recently, as I waited to have my prostate biopsy, she has told me a number of times that it is not to be worried about. I do anyway, as I am still mortal and human with human emotions. Other spiritual beings have said the same thing to me. These beings do know what goes on in the physical world. God knows absolutely everything.

It is love that flows freely through the veil that separates the spirit world from the physical realm. It is love that allows communication from those who have departed to those who still remain. There have been many times since Marilyn's death and more so lately due to my prostate cancer that I have felt and seen the wings of a gorgeous angel wrapping around me in such a loving way. At the same time, the angel puts her head next to me in such a loving way that it is almost too beautiful to describe. And at the same time this is happening, I can still perceive the presence of my late wife in her white blouse and blue skirt standing a few feet away, loving me and giving me encouragement to continue on through this trial with cancer that I currently face. By the way, the angel who wraps her wings around me has blond hair and blue eyes.

God also provides us what we need while we remain in this life. I have a wonderful fiancé that is my lifelong companion that will be by my side until one of us goes back to our spiritual home. She has gotten the nod of approval from the spiritual beings I have contact with, including Marilyn. Her name means "bringer of good news." It is in these ways that God wants to comfort all of us when we have difficulties and hardship and suffering, which is our lot on this earth. All one needs to do is to completely open their eyes, open their minds, and especially open their hearts and believe that everything I have just said is true, for this is part of the nature of God's creation for our benefit.

Through my visits to heaven, I have come to know that there are multiple levels of heaven. Each one is inhabited by those beings who have accomplished a certain level of spiritual closeness to God. As we learn more and more about God and as we grow in our spiritual nature, we become more and more like God and more and more wish to be like our Father and our Mother in heaven. If we pursue this path, we will find ourselves very much less connected to the material things in life. The material things in life fall away from us as meaningful goals in our life. What become more important are the loving relationships that we form with other people. What we become more interested in is the ability to help others achieve their spiritual goals and help them move away from the trappings of the material world, which has unfortunately ensnared so many millions of people.

I believe that God will give them another chance. But this I do not know for sure. I do not know how many chances God will give those who have not progressed in their spiritual life, becoming closer and closer to him in the spiritual realm. I know there must come a time in which enough is enough and they will have sentenced themselves to live in eternity at a distance from God. And once they know the truth that they have been denying throughout all their existences in the spirit realm, they will realize that they have missed the most wonderful opportunity throughout all creation. Then they will begin wailing and gnashing their teeth, knowing that they will no longer be able to approach God as others already have through the spiritual opportunities God gives each of us every day of our lives. This is one definition of hell I believe. Billy Graham, the great evangelist of the last fifty years, has always said that hell for him is being cut off from God and not being able to feel his presence within his life. I believe this is a good definition of hell. I too have had times in my life when God seems not to be with me. Normally, I can sense His loving presence if I just calm down, flush out all the brain chatter that each of us has and then with complete love and reverence, pray a simple mantra, "Open unto thee dear Lord, open unto thee." This is my favorite mantra, and I c use even this when I give Reiki sessions.

So I believe, through my mystical experiences, prayer life, meditations, and education in reading hundreds of books, there are two distinct realms of God's creation that we are allowed to perceive. There may be many more that I have not been exposed to. But this I do not know. But what I do know is there is an inexorable connection between the physical world and the spiritual world. It is this inexorable connection of love that allows the spiritual world to assist those of us in the physical world. Keep on the right direction according to God's will for each of us. If we do this and if we pay attention to what God tells us through many different ways, one of which is direct mystical experience, we will know that we are on the right track and that we are doing God's will for us and growing spiritually as he has willed for each of us where we ultimately will become so close to God that it will be hard to determine where God begins and we end. Imagine what ecstasy that must be like.

The rapturous ecstasy that we will receive constantly is something that none of us can envision at this time but is something that we will experience if we just follow God's will and continually ask for his guidance and act accordingly. For God wishes each of us to be in constant commune with Him and God our Mother in such a way that all in rapturous ecstasy for all eternity. This is my prayer for you, and I hope this book that you have read has brought you closer to God and will propel you on your path, your spiritual path as God has chosen for you, to bring you closer to Him and experience the eternal rapturous ecstasy that He wishes to give each of His children. May God bless each of you and your families.

About the Author

This is an outstanding and groundbreaking book. It is the first book that dares to reveal just how divine mystical experiences actually feel like to the person receiving them—the physical sensations, as well as the mental and emotional experiences. Richard has been one of the children of God who has experienced hundreds of divine experiences. He describes how divine mystical experiences fit into our lives and especially what we can learn about God through them. The wondrous love of God for all his children is sometimes visited upon us in the form of different kinds of mystical experiences that bring with them indescribable and pleasurable sensations along with deep understandings of the spirit world. These events are direct gifts from God. They come unexpectedly and can improve your life in ways that can only be dreamed about. All we have to do is to be open to God to enter our lives, and wonderful things such as mystical experiences will start to happen for our benefit.

His first occurred in a jet over the Pacific Ocean. Since then, experiencing the divine has become a regular and normal part of his life. Some have come to Richard unexpectedly, and others have come during meditation sessions. All have been ever so pleasurable and reveal new information that could not be obtained any other way. These divine experiences are real, and Richard says no one should ever fear the occurrences of these divine experiences. They are so loving and warm feeling that you do not want them to end. Thus these experiences are so much like our understanding that God loves unconditionally. In this book he shares just how it actually feels like to receive divine mystical gifts, the lessons and information they can bring with them, and how they will improve your life.

About the Author

Richard has become a spiritual authority and enjoys working with people to improve their prayer lives. He holds a degree in chemistry, a minor in philosophy, a master's degree in business, and a master's degree in pastoral ministry emphasizing spirituality. He is a Reiki master and has helped many people with a variety of problems. He also holds a commercial pilot's license and flight instructor rating and has owned several high-performance aircraft. In the past, he also worked as a real estate broker, which allowed him to retire early and concentrate on his first love, which is pursuing an ever-increasing understanding and love of God our Father.

He has worked at NASA in the planetary branch, studying extraterrestrial particles in the upper atmosphere. He has continued to study such topics as astronomy, the latest developments in quantum physics, and other scientific pursuits. Rich knows that the physical world represented by scientific inquiry and the spiritual world represented by theology are two realms of existence in God's creation that are inexorably intertwined for the benefit of his children. There is a pervasive unity that characterizes all creation, and mankind is finally just starting to understand this. Talking to Richard in person is an unforgettable experience.

Made in the USA
San Bernardino, CA
30 January 2015